CASH
TRAPS

Other Books by Jeff Davidson

Breathing Space: Living & Working at a Comfortable Pace in a Sped-Up Society (Master Media, 1992)

35 Ways to Make Your Bank Work for You (Consumer Reports Books, 1992)

The Domino Effect: How to Grow Sales, Profits, and Market Share Through Super Vision, by Don Vlcek with Jeff Davidson (Business One–Irwin, 1991)

Marketing to Home-Based Businesses (Business One–Irwin, 1991)

You Can Start Your Own Business (Washington Publications, 1991)

Power and Protocol for Getting to the Top (Shapolsky, 1991)

Avoiding the Pitfalls of Starting Your Own Business (Shapolsky, 1991)

Blow Your Own Horn: How to Get Ahead and Get Noticed (Berkley, 1991)

Selling to the Giants: How to Become a Key Supplier to Large Corporations (Tab/McGraw-Hill, 1991)

How to Have a Good Year Every Year, Dave Yoho and Jeff Davidson (Berkley, 1991)

Marketing Your Consulting and Professional Services (Wiley, 1990)

Marketing for the Home-Based Business (Bob Adams, Inc., 1990)

The Marketing Sourcebook for Small Business (Wiley, 1989)

Marketing on a Shoestring (Wiley, 1988)

Getting New Clients (Wiley, 1987)

How to Be a "Ten" in Business, Don Beveridge and Jeff Davidson (Business One–Irwin, 1987)

Marketing Your Community (Public Technology, 1987)

Checklist Management (National Press, 1987)

CASH
TRAPS:

Small Business Secrets
for Reducing Costs
and Improving Cash Flow

Jeffrey P. Davidson
and Charles W. Dean

John Wiley & Sons

New York • Chichester • Brisbane • Toronto • Singapore

Published by John Wiley & Sons, Inc.

Library of Congress Cataloging-in-Publication Data

Davidson, Jeffrey P.
    Cash traps : small business secrets for reducing costs and
improving cash flow / by Jeffrey P. Davidson and Charles W. Dean.
        p.   cm.
    Includes bibliographical references (p.   ) and index.
    ISBN 0-471-53625-3 (alk. paper).—ISBN 0-471-53624-5 (pbk. :
alk. paper)
    1. Small business—Cash position.   2. Cash flow.   I. Dean,
Charles W., 1944–   . II. Title.
HG4028.C45D38   1992
658.15′244—dc20   91-16354

Printed in the United States of America

10 9 8 7 6 5 4 3 2 1

Printed and bound by Courier Companies, Inc.

Dedication

Jeff Davidson dedicates this book to the people and institutions who helped him avoid cash traps early in his career, including Emanuel Davidson, Mechanics Savings Bank, Hartford National Bank and Trust, Society for Savings, Ford Motor Credit, Shirley Davidson, American Federal Savings Bank, Bonita Nelson, Martin Schor, Peter Morabito, Ellen Schor, Susan Millard Davidson, and Chuck Dean.

Charles W. Dean dedicates this book to Helen P. Dean, who taught him the value of work and the importance of asking questions.

Acknowledgments

The authors wish to acknowledge several individuals for their subject matter expertise or support. Willis Shen handled the preliminary research and prepared the index. Ed Wong offered expert proofreading assistance. Kelly Leahy Simpson and Kathleen Reynolds helped with the writing of selected chapters. William Elsey spearheaded an earlier project which identified techniques for business energy reduction. The U.S. Small Business Administration's fine cash-flow form and booklet on insurance coverage bolstered the text, as did Dun & Bradstreet's source materials on collections and credit ratings.

Thanks also to the talented crew at John Wiley & Sons including Karl Weber, Neal Maillet, Peter Clifton, Richard McCullough, Audrey Melkin and Joan O'Neil.

CONTENTS

FOREWORD

It is expensive to be in business today; if you run your own company, division, or department, you are already acutely aware of how expensive it can be. While U.S. Government statistics officially indicate that inflation is down, the reality for you and several million other entrepreneurs is that the costs of operating a business—from labor to inventory, from supplies to utilities, from warehousing to banking, from insurance to collections— all continue to creep up at an annoying, if not steep, rate.

Keeping operating expenses at reasonable levels has assumed greater and greater importance in recent years, and conserving cash is no less important than making more sales. But where do you turn for guidance? The standard books on financial management offer a plethora of financial assessments you can make, ratios you can calculate, and formulas you can follow, presumably so that you know exactly where you stand financially. This is all well and good, but what specific action steps can you take right *Now* to stem an inordinate flow of dollars out your doors?

Enter *Cash Traps: Small Business Secrets for Reducing Costs and Improving Cash Flow* by Jeff Davidson and Chuck Dean. Davidson and Dean cut right to the quick with practical insights and recommendations that you can put into action. They don't waste any time or words in conveying to you surefire, proven techniques for staying liquid, getting leaner, and keeping more of your cash.

After *briefly* reviewing the fundamentals of preparing a cashflow analysis, they launch right into money-saving techniques in the crucial and high-cost areas of payroll, purchasing, and utilities. They tackle working with bankers, reducing the insurance bite, and collecting more effectively. They also cover managing the checkbook, making more sensible bids on jobs, and employing self-auditing techniques.

To aid you in getting through the book, each chapter concludes with a section called "Hot Tips and Insights." I found this feature to be particularly appealing. The few charts and tables included in the book convey a great deal of information; yet they can be easily grasped.

As I was reading this valuable book, I was struck by cash traps I've encountered in my own business—making retail equipment purchases at top dollar, running up excess mailing costs, and overpaying for some types of insurance.

Regardless of the type of business you're in, I'm confident that you'll gain a wealth of ideas for retaining more of your dollars, whether it's reviewing your telephone systems, reducing core staff while increasing supplemental staff, making profitable bids on new projects or contracts, or simply paying bills when it's most advantageous for you.

I hope you find *Cash Traps* to be just what you need—a clear and uncomplicated approach to retaining more of your richly deserved earnings.

Nicholas Kalis, Publisher
Kalis' Shopping Center Leasing Directory

INTRODUCTION

It's difficult today to stay out of cash traps and keep operating expenses down. As consumers, we've become used to having things always cost a little more than anticipated and then paying for them with plastic. As executives and entrepreneurs, with responsibilities for running a department or a business, we learn early in our careers that sometimes, despite the most carefully laid plans, costly and unexpected situations and events crop up *beyond* those we had already generously allocated for.

The term, *Cash Traps*, as used in this book, will refer to any situation in which you must part with out-of-pocket dollars to keep a business viable. Cash traps can occur when you pay too much for items or when the price is right but your funds are tight.

Cash traps include both short-term crises and routine expenses that may drain your working capital. Diverse activities such as making payroll, purchasing, and paying excessive energy, phone, and other utility bills are all cash traps, as are over-paying for insurance coverage, receiving bad checks, and employee theft.

Holding on to dead inventory is a cash trap. So too, potentially, is making unprofitable bids on jobs you might win. The capital required to sustain an effective marketing campaign, install an upgraded accounting system, or undergo store remodeling is *always* greater than first estimated, and in many cases is more than double. Imprudent purchasing is perhaps the biggest cash trap of all.

Every business, even the most successful, faces cash traps at various times in the course of operations. Some develop preventative and precautionary measures to minimize their occurrence or effect. Too many businesses scramble to put out one cash trap fire after another.

*This book is about preventative and precautionary mea-
sures, as well as on-the-spot remedies you can use to protect
your cash flow, shave dollars off your operating expenses,
keep yourself liquid more of the time, and thus improve
overall operations.*

Everything Costs.   Today, it's expensive to be alive, let alone to
run a successful business, but who wants to contemplate the
alternatives? Whenever you overlook forthcoming expense items,
you can run into a potential cash trap. The cost of maintenance
and repair of key equipment can sneak up on you. When you are
looking for new staff, the search process, with classified advertisements, search fees, and related costs can quickly become an
expensive proposition, rapidly climbing into the four- and then
five-figure range.

Every time you add another piece of equipment or office device, a whole host of costs come into play, beyond the cost of
the item itself. Take the simple, harmless, bargain-priced fax
machine you bought recently. Adding another phone line for
your fax machine yields new installation charges, monthly
charges, and long-distance charges. Then there's the thermal paper, storage, message distribution, and record-keeping—a whole
new set of expenses—line-item expenses and attendant human
resource costs.

In mid-July, when you plan the budget for the next fiscal year,
who thinks about, or wants to think about, the cost of snow
removal from the employee parking lot? Okay, you say, removing
the snow from the parking lot is a minor expense of being in
business. *The problem is that minor expenses are flourishing.*
Throw in an increased fee for office cleaning; add a few more
dollars for electricity rate hikes reflected on your energy bill; and
then toss in the cost of repairing a leaky roof that just made itself
known.

We know of businesses that annually pay more for express-
mail services than for regular mail, and the product they furnish
isn't regarded as urgent by any of the customers.

A growing roster of bad debts and collection expenses can be
a crusher to your business and put a choke-hold on your cash

flow. Employee pilferage, never mind customer theft, IS at epidemic proportions and no business is immune.

What about those nitpicking costs charged by the banks and others? Every time a check is returned or bounced, you are looking at $15.00 to $25.00. On a lesser note, what about the directories, reference books, and handbooks you refer to that all need to be updated?

Sacred Dollars

If you operate on a thin net profit margin, say 2 to 3 percent, even a relatively small savings of $300 is significant. With a 2 percent net profit margin, you'd have to sell $15,000 in goods to generate a $300 net profit before taxes.

In every business, regardless of its profit margin, *dollars conserved contribute to a multiplier effect*, freeing you from having to generate that much more in sales. Consequently, we will introduce cash conservation principles and techniques for trimming operating expenses of varying magnitudes. Our approach in helping you to avoid cash traps is to treat the dollars you can retain as sacred.

What This Book Is Not

Cash Traps is not a primer for first-time managers or entrepreneurs. We won't burden you with finely printed formulae, or with more than a few simple charts, forms, or equations. We won't stop and explain basic financial terminology.

We don't discuss setting up ledgers or installing financial systems, and we will not cover tax ramifications. We also will not discuss financial analysis techniques such as plotting sources and uses of funds or undertaking intricate ratio analyses, which don't help you when you are faced with a miserable working capital position. Further, we are not offering a panacea for your financial woes—after all is said and done, tighter expense control coupled with more profitable sales is usually the best antidote for an ailing cash position.

The book *will* offer encouraging, actionable advice to keep you from spending more than necessary. In reader-friendly prose, we'll discuss strategies you can follow and steps you can take to keep your operations liquid and to reduce the tide of expenses that drain dollars from your company.

Chapter 1, "Maintaining a Positive Cash Flow," offers a quick look at some of the nuances in preparing, maintaining, and using cash-flow projections. We'll discuss the need for conservatism, contingencies, buffers, and getting at the roots of your cash-flow problems. As we'll see, there's a lot more involved than just collecting your earnings faster. Chapter 2, "Pruning Your Payroll Costs," offers a variety of techniques for keeping payroll costs as low as possible without sacrificing quality and productivity. Techniques include converting payroll periods, creating core and supplemental staff, using contractors and work-for-hire employees, along with others, and other methods for reducing payroll cost.

In Chapter 3, "Prudent Purchasing," we'll discuss why the high cost of goods sold can be the single greatest expense for most businesses, particularly those that buy raw materials for resale. We'll then review purchasing techniques used by the masters, including peak buying, odd-lot purchasing, commercial discounts, and shopping at superstores and auctions.

In Chapter 4, "Reducing Utility, Phone and Postage Costs," we'll tackle three expense areas that have risen dramatically. First, we'll highlight the cumulative effect of lights, equipment, machinery, and other energy-consuming devices, and then discuss how simple techniques and equipment changes will quickly pay for themselves and yield substantial benefits thereafter. Then we'll offer sound advice for getting the phone system you want and for lowering phone bills, and we'll review low-cost mailing options instead of over-relying on high-priced express mail services.

"Getting the Most from Your Bank," the subject of Chapter 5, illuminates how to interact successfully with banks and other financial institutions. From lower interest loans to financial planning services, you will be able to make considerable financial headway in dealing with banks by following the advice in this chapter. Chapter 6, "Minimizing Your Risk": Most businesses are overinsured in some areas and underinsured in others. This chapter reveals the coverage you need, some alternatives to traditional insurance, and strategies for reducing both risk and premiums.

Not receiving the money you've already earned from customers is enough to make you scream. In Chapter 7, "Collecting Your Cash," we'll lay out simple systems and timely advice on how to put muscle into your collection efforts. Chapter 8, "Checkbook Techniques and Tips," covers the basics of managing your check-writing and offers safeguards you'll want to know about. It also introduces software programs and other innovative arrangements to reduce the cost of check processing in general.

Chapter 9, "Contractor Cash Traps," offers keen insights into how to avoid cash traps, starting from the bidding process itself. It reviews break-even analysis and also covers various ways contractors can maintain a positive cash flow, including front-loaded billing, progress payments, customer financing, and the like. Read this chapter even if you're not a contractor because many of the principles discussed and recommendations offered have wide applicability within other lines of business.

The final chapter, Chapter 10: "Self-Auditing Techniques," offers a series of checklists you can use to help ensure your internal systems for handling cash, checks, and other moneys are air-tight. Unfortunately, the opportunity and temptation among some employees to siphon cash is often irresistible. Aggregate figures on employee theft are enough to make any manager lose sleep. We will examine a variety of measures you can employ to safeguard your cash management system.

When you've finished this book, you'll have more than enough areas in which you can get started right away to head off cash traps and maintain a stronger cash-flow position.

1

MAINTAINING A POSITIVE CASH FLOW

It is better to have a permanent income than be fascinating.

Oscar Wilde

Even when their businesses are running at full capacity and their staffs are swamped with work, many owners and managers find it an ongoing struggle to pay the monthly bills.

It doesn't matter whether your product is superior to the competition's, or that you've earned a sparkling reputation in your field, or even that you're in such demand you have to turn customers away. If your cash flow is always tight, you're headed for trouble. When you're continually strapped for cash, you lower the expectations and energy of even your most loyal staff and dissipate the confidence others have in you.

Besides leaving you with little or no safety buffer, a weak cash flow also prevents you from innovating. Medium-cost marketing opportunities are out of range; suddenly, only shoestring techniques seem feasible. You operate with the fear that something will go wrong, and if something does, you hope it won't be too costly. You take the path of least resistance, accepting the status quo and its inherent disadvantages in a rapidly changing world.

With little cash in reserve, maintenance routines slip. You spend more time on the phone explaining your slow payments than you do making more revenue. Self-doubt creeps into the picture: "Why can't I (or we) break away from these cash traps?" You fear certain dates on the calendar such as when quarterly tax payments must be filed, monthly rents are owed, or the weekly payroll is due.

When things really start to go sour, you begin screening calls you used to take before. You start looking for short cuts. You overprice, then underprice your goods or services. You start to ignore certain expenses. You fantasize about winning the lottery or the trifecta. You begin to consider what to sell off. You hustle into and out of the office and avoid looking at people directly, particularly your staff.

If all this goes on for too long, you ruminate about dropping out—just leaving one day for the tropics, with no clues as to your whereabouts. Sleep, when you can get it, is your only real relief. You start to examine turning points in your life to try to uncover some recurring, fatal flaw. You make excuses you never thought you'd hear yourself say, like it's the fault of the market, or the government, or the customers, or the competition, or the breaks.

The list goes on and on. You can't pay competitive wages to your staff and so the quality of your output drops. Your customers become dissatisfied. You have no money to correct problems. And you're out of business. Or worse, you make the business hang on, operating in a living death mode.

BALANCING INFLOWS AND OUTFLOWS

As you know too well, your business can be making a profit, but the larger the profit, potentially the more pronounced your cash-flow problems and difficulty you face meeting expenses can become. Often you have to pay cash to make a product or supply a service before your customers pay the bill. Expenses are incurred before income is received. Over time, in a profitable business your cash inflows should begin to outpace your outflows and put you in a liquid position.

What happens, however, is that as cash becomes available, the same diligence and frugality exhibited in lean times is not maintained. Moreover, as business expands, the task of balancing inflows with unprecedented outlays to finance growth becomes challenging.

THE CASH-FLOW PROJECTION

The easiest way to stay abreast of your cash flow is simply to plot it, manually if you have to or with any of the marvelous spreadsheet programs, such as Lotus 1-2-3, Quatro, Visicalc, Multiplan, or Plan Perfect. The most frequent projections undertaken are by month for 12 months or by quarter for many years. Loan officers and investors seek one-year projections by month and three- to five-year projections by quarter.

A well-developed cash-flow projection pinpoints the timing and magnitude of cash needs. It is a forecast of funds a business anticipates receiving, on the one hand, and disbursing, on the other. Over a given time span, it plots the anticipated cash position at specific times.

While you may not want to see them show up on your projection spreadsheet, a cash-flow projection pinpoints deficiencies in cash from the amount necessary to efficiently operate the business. You should always want to know when you are headed for a shortfall: forewarned is forearmed. Conversely, if cash excesses are forecasted, they might indicate excessive borrowing or idle money that could be put to work.

The form presented in Figure 1.1, with which you're likely to be familiar, enables you to record both estimates of cash receipts and expenditures and actual totals as they become known— hence the two columns, "estimate" and "actual." Not all of the line item classifications listed on the form will match your business, so you'll need to make some modifications.

As you project and plot each cash inflow and outflow, we hope your cash position at the end of each month will be positive. Otherwise, you've got your work cut out for you. Postponing a purchase or speeding up some collections may be enough to convert a negative cash balance for one month into a positive one.

12-Month Cash-Flow Projection Form

YEAR　　　　　　　　　MONTH	Pre-Start-up Position		1		2		3		12		TOTAL Columns 1–12		
	Estimate	Actual	Estimate	Actual	Estimate	Actual	Estimate	Actual	Estimate	Actual	Estimate	Actual	
1. CASH ON HAND (Beginning of month)													1
2. CASH RECEIPTS (a) Cash Sales													2 (a)
(b) Collections from Credit Accounts													(b)
(c) Loan or Other Cash injection (Specify)													(c)
3. TOTAL CASH RECEIPTS (2a + 2b + 2c = 3)													3
4. TOTAL CASH AVAILABLE (Before cash out) (1 + 3)													4
5. CASH PAID OUT (a) Purchases (Merchandise)													5 (a)
(b) Gross Wages (Excludes withdrawals)													(b)
(c) Payroll Expenses (Taxes, etc.)													(c)
(d) Outside Services													(d)
(e) Supplies (Office and operating)													(e)
(f) Repairs and Maintenance													(f)
(g) Advertising													(g)
(h) Car, Delivery, and Travel													(h)
(i) Accounting and Legal													(i)
(j) Rent													(j)
(k) Telephone													(k)
(l) Utilities													(l)
(m) Insurance													(m)
(n) Taxes (Real estate, etc.)													(n)
(o) Interest													(o)
(p) Other Expenses (Specify each)													(p)
(q) Miscellaneous (Unspecified)													(q)
(r) Subtotal													(r)
(s) Loan Principal Payment													(s)
(t) Capital Purchases (Specify)													(t)
(u) Other Start-up Costs													(u)
(v) Reserve and/or Escrow (Specify)													(v)
(w) Owner's Withdrawal													(w)
6. TOTAL CASH PAID OUT (Total 5a thru 5w)													6
7. CASH POSITION (End of month) (4 minus 6)													7

Figure 1.1.

Table 1.1 explains the various components of the twelve-month cash-flow projection sheet.

12-Month Cash-Flow Projection Sheet

1. Cash on Hand

Beginning of month—cash on hand equals cash position of the previous month (No. 7).

2. Cash Receipts

　　a.　Cash Sales—all cash sales; omit credit sales unless cash is actually received.

12-Month Cash-Flow Projection Sheet

b.   Collections from Credit Accounts—amount to be received from all credit accounts.

c.   Loan or Other Cash Injection—indicate here all cash injections not shown in 2a or 2b above.

3. Total Cash Receipts

2a + 2b + 2c = 3—self explanatory.

4. Total Cash Available

Before cash out (1 + 3)—self explanatory.

5. Cash Paid Out

a.   Purchases—merchandise for resale or for use in product, paid for in current month.

b.   Gross Wages (excludes withdrawals)—base pay plus overtime, if any.

c.   Payroll Expenses (taxes, etc.)—includes paid vacations, paid sick leave, health insurance, unemployment insurance, etc. (this might equal from 20 to 45 percent of 5b).

d.   Outside Services—this could include outside labor and/or material for specialized or overflow work, including subcontracting.

e.   Supplies (office and operating)—items purchased for use in the business, not for resale.

f.   Repairs and Maintenance—include periodic large expenditures such as painting or decorating.

g.   Advertising—this amount should be adequate to maintain sales volume and includes telephone book yellow pages cost.

h.   Car, Delivery, and Travel—if personal car is used, charge in this column, including parking.

i.   Accounting and Legal—outside services including, for example, bookkeeping.

j.   Rent—payment for commercial space.

k.   Telephone—self-explanatory.

l.   Utilities—water, heat, light, and/or power.

12-Month Cash-Flow Projection Sheet

m. Insurance—coverage on business property and products; e.g., fire, liability, workers' compensation, fidelity, etc.

n. Taxes—real estate, plus inventory tax, sales tax, or excise tax, if applicable.

o. Interest—interest on loans (see 2c).

p. Other Expenses (specify each)—unexpected expenditures may be included here as a safety factor.

q. Miscellaneous (unspecified)—small expenditures for which separate accounts would not be practical.

r. Subtotal—this subtotal indicates cash out for operating costs.

s. Loan Principal Payment—include payment on all loans, including vehicle and equipment purchases on time payment.

t. Capital Purchases—nonexpensed, depreciable expenditures such as equipment, building, vehicle purchases, and leasehold improvements.

u. Other Start-up Costs—expenses incurred prior to first-month projections and paid for after the "start up" position.

v. Reserve and/or Escrow—example: insurance, tax, or equipment escrow to reduce impact of large periodic payments.

w. Owner's Withdrawal—payment for owner's income tax, social security, health insurance, executive life insurance premiums, etc.

6. **Total Cash Paid Out**

Total 5a through 5w.

7. **Cash Position**

End of month (4-6)—enter this amount in "1. Cash on Hand" box for the following month.

Table 1.1.

A Major Caveat.   It isn't difficult to produce a detailed cash-flow projection which is off by thousands if not tens of thousands of dollars. The assumptions made about the projected cash inflows and outflows are as important as the actual figures themselves. For example, unexpected developments in any one of the following areas could potentially throw off your projections by considerable amounts:

- Growth rates
- Tax rates
- Time periods required
- Production facilities
- Environmental conditions
- General economic conditions
- Contracts to be negotiated
- Competitors' actions
- Employee turnover
- Capital expenditures
- Breakdowns
- Interdependence

Nevertheless, if you hone and refine as you go along and keep extending your cash-flow analysis by another month or another quarter, as another month or quarter rolls by, you can gain an excellent handle on where your dollars are coming from and going to. Probably the major benefit of maintaining an updated cash flow is that you are able to reduce (but surely not eliminate) the number of surprises you encounter. Software spreadsheet programs help simplify calculations, but there is no substitute for the accurate input of original data.

If you have been in business for several years, you can draw upon previous revenue and expense data to help you in making projections (see the next section, Revenue Forecasting). It's always useful to refer to financial sourcebooks that reveal the typical operating costs, composite balance sheets, and profit-and-loss statements of other businesses in your industry.

A good source is *RMA Annual Statement Studies*, published by Robert Morris Associates, Philadelphia National Bank Building, Philadelphia, PA 19107. *Annual Statement Studies* can be used for general guidelines, but not for absolute industry norms because the financial statements presented are not selected by any random or statistically reliable method.

Another good source of financial information is Dun and Bradstreet's *Cost of Doing Business*, which draws upon statistics of income prepared by the statistics division of the Internal Revenue Service. Three separate pamphlets are prepared for proprietorships, partnerships, and corporations. The number of firms used in the total sample size are indicated for each line of business. The *Cost of Doing Business* can be obtained by writing to: Economic Analysis Department, Dun and Bradstreet Corporation, 299 Park Avenue, New York, NY 10171.

Another source is *The Almanac of Business and Industrial Financial Ratios*, by Leo Troy, Ph.D., published by Prentice Hall, Inc., Englewood Cliffs, NJ 07632. The *Almanac* also relies upon data from the Internal Revenue Service. A key feature is that financial data is presented for 12 different sizes of assets, ranging from under $100,000 to over $250,000,000.

The *Almanac* supplies current performance facts and figures, and aids in answering many cost-related questions such as, "Compared to the industry as a whole and to companies of a similar size, how well is my company doing in controlling costs?" Or "What percentage of sales goes to pensions or other benefit plans?" Or "How do my company's outlays on compensation of officers, rents, repairs, and advertising compare with others?"

The local office of the Small Business Administration can provide a series of reports on expenses as a percent of sales for several different lines of business. You may also draw on information supplied by the association or professional trade group serving your industry. William Cohen, in his book, *The Entrepreneur and Small Business Problem Solver* (Wiley, 2nd edition, 1990), presents a variety of associations that have published operating ratios and financial norms for firms in their respective industries (see Figure 1.2).

American Association of Advertising Agencies, 666 Third Avenue, 13th Floor, New York, NY 10017

American Camping Association, 5000 State Road, 67N, Martinsville, IN 46151

American Financial Services Association, 1101 14th Street, NW, Washington, DC 20005

American Jewelry Marketing Association, 1900 Arch Street, Philadelphia, PA 19103

American Meat Institute, P.O. Box 3556, Washington, DC 20007

American Paper Institute, 260 Madison Avenue, New York, NY 10016

American Society of Association Executives, 1575 Eye Street, NW, Washington, DC 20005

American Supply Association, 20 North Wacker Drive, Suite 2260, Chicago, IL 60606

Bowling Proprietors Association of America, Box 5802, Arlington, TX 76011

Building Owners and Managers Association, International, 1250 Eye Street, NW, Suite 200, Washington, DC 20005

Door and Hardware Institute, 7711 Old Springhouse Road, McLean, VA 22102

Florists' Transworld Delivery Association/Interflora, 29200 Northwestern Highway, Southfield, MI 48037

Food Market Institute, Inc., 1750 K Street, NW, Suite 700, Washington, DC 20006

Foodservice Equipment Distributors Association, 332 South Michigan Avenue, Chicago, IL 60604

Mechanical Contractors Association of America, 5410 Grosvenor Lane, Suite 120, Bethesda, MD 20814

Menswear Retailers of America, 2011 Eye Street, NW, Washington, DC 20006

Motor and Equipment Manufacturers' Association, P.O. Box 1638, 300 Sylvan Avenue, Englewood Cliffs, NJ 07632

National American Wholesale Grocers' Association, 201 Park Washington Court, Falls Church, VA 22046

National Appliance and Radio–TV Dealers Association, 10 East 22nd Street, Lombard, IL 60148

National Art Materials Trade Association, 178 Lakeview Avenue, Clifton, NJ 07011

National Association of Accountants, P.O. Box 433, 10 Paragon Drive, Montvale, NJ 07645

National Association of Electrical Distributors, 28 Cross Street, Norwalk, CT 06851

National Association of Food Chains, 1750 K Street, Suite 700, Washington, DC 20006

Figure 1.2. **(Continued)**

National Association of Furniture Manufacturers, P.O. Box HP.7, High Point, NC 27261

National Association of Textile and Apparel Distributors, P.O. Box 1325, Melbourne, FL 32902

National Association of Tobacco Distributors, 1199 North Fairfax Street, Suite 701, Alexandria, VA 22314

National Automatic Merchandising Association, 20 North Wacker Drive, Chicago, IL 60606

National Beer Wholesalers Association, 5205 Leesburg Pike, Suite 505, Falls Church, VA 22041

National Confectioners Association of the United States, 645 North Michigan Avenue, Suite 1006, Chicago, IL 60611

National Decorating Products Association, 1050 North Linbergh Boulevard, St. Louis, MO 63132

National Electrical Contractors Association, Inc., 7315 Wisconsin Avenue, Bethesda, MD 20814

National Electrical Manufacturers Association, 2101 L Street, NW, Washington, DC 20037

National Farm and Power Equipment Dealers Association, 10877 Watson Road, P.O. Box 8517, St. Louis, MO 63826

National Grocers Association, 1825 Samuel Moore Drive, Reston, VA 22090

National Home Furnishings Association, 220 West Gerry Lane, Wood Dale, IL 60191

National Kitchen Cabinet Association., P.O. Box 6830, Falls Church, VA 22046

National Lumber and Building Material Dealers Association, 40 Ivy Street, SE, Washington, DC 20003

National Machine Tool Builders Association, 7901 Westpark Drive, McLean, VA 22102

National Office Products Association, 301 North Fairfax Street, Alexandria, VA 22314

National Restaurant Association, 311 First Street, NW, Washington, DC 20001

National Retail Hardware Association, 770 North High School Road, Indianapolis, IN 46214

National Retail Merchants Association, 100 West 31st Street, New York, NY 10001

National Shoe Retailers Association, 9861 Broken Land Parkway, Columbia, MD 21046

National Soft Drink Association, 1101 16th Street, NW, Washington, DC 20036

Figure 1.2.   **(Continued)**

National Sporting Goods Association, Lake Center Plaza Building, 1699 Wall Street, Mount Prospect, IL 60056

National Tire Dealers and Retreaders Association, 1250 Eye Street, NW, Suite 400, Washington, DC 20005

National Wholesale Druggists' Association, 105 Oronoco Street, P.O. Box 238, Alexandria, VA 22313

National Wholesale Hardware Association, 1900 Arch Street, Philadelphia, PA 19103

North American Heating and Airconditioning Wholesalers Association, P.O. Box 16790, 1389 Dublin Road, Columbus, OH 43216

Northeastern Retail Lumbermens Association, 339 East Avenue, Rochester, NY 14604

Optical Laboratories Association, P.O. Box 2000, Merrifield, VA 22116

Painting and Decorating Contractors of America, 7223 Lee Highway, Falls Church, VA 22046

Petroleum Equipment Institute, P.O. Box 2380, Tulsa, OK 74104

Petroleum Marketers Association, 1120 Vermont Avenue, Suite 1130, Washington, DC 20005

Printing Industries of America, Inc., 1730 North Lynn Street, Arlington, VA 22209

Scientific Apparatus Makers Association, 1101 16th Street, NW, Washington, DC 20036

Shoe Service Institute of America, 112 Calendar Court Mall, La Grange, IL 60525

Society of the Plastics Industry, Inc., The, 1275 K Street, NW, Suite 400, Washington, DC 20005

United Fresh Fruit and Vegetable Association, 727 North Washington Street, Alexandria, VA 22314

Figure 1.2. Selected Business Associations (From Cohen, William, Ph.D., *The Entrepreneur and Small Business Problem Solver*, 2nd edition. New York: Wiley, 1990. Reprinted by permission.)

In addition to information gleaned from sources such as those cited above, good cash-flow preparation also entails lots of assumptions, estimates, and just plain guesswork.

Considerable Time Up Front, Time Savings Thereafter. Although you can probably construct a crude cash-flow projection in a few hours, it can take several days to construct a detailed, well-researched cash-flow projection that reflects well-founded market assumptions, resulting revenues, and all expenses—cash outflows—associated with operating the business.

Once your cash-flow projection is up and operative, modify it as time passes. Rolling over the months to maintain a 12-month projection need not take more than a couple hours a week. That's not an inordinate time investment considering the valuable information you receive and the new-found measure of financial planning and control you will enjoy.

The cash-flow analysis is among the most comprehensive of the many other financial planning tools, yet it is the easiest to read and understand. It's the one financial planning tool we see as mandatory for successful operations of businesses of all sizes.

In his book, *How to Have a Good Year, Every Year*, Dave Yoho discusses how, unfortunately, too many business owners and managers operate out of their checkbook without adequate cash-flow planning. This is characterized by the company or individual who sees a fair amount of money in the checkbook and then decides to make a purchase—in a reckless way of managing finances.

These managers are stung every time some equipment needs repair or an unexpected but necessary expense arises, because they have no cash-flow analysis to which to refer. If they have a working cash-flow budget for each month, they could quickly determine whether the funds were available for an unplanned purchase.

Yoho observes that the typical checkbook manager is frequently juggling finances and withholding payments to suppliers. This type of manager ends up paying the most for needed goods and services, because he or she is dealing from a position of weakness.

A Multifaceted Approach. The effort to maintain a positive cash flow and keep operating expenses in check needs to be multifaceted and unrelenting. It involves anticipating when timing gaps between cash inflows and outflows may occur, vigorously reducing waste and unnecessary expense, striving for greater productivity from your staff, collecting money due you as soon as possible, cultivating relationships with those who can advance you needed debt or equity capital, and treating every dollar that comes and goes as a quintessential, vital liquid asset.

REVENUE FORECASTING

The top part of the cash-flow analysis calls for revenue forecasting. Some managers who are crackerjack at maintaining a watchful eye over cash outflows and plotting them accordingly for some reason let revenue forecasting slide.

A man whom we'll call Bill Hodges ran a 16-person graphics and design firm serving major corporate accounts. Bill's "method" of revenue forecasting was to give mental recognition to eight to ten potential contracts looming on the horizon at varying dollar figures. During a consulting engagement with Bill, we learned that his system for revenue forecasting was not even roughed out on scratch paper or discussed with anyone else. Understandably, Bill's system was of little value in effectively managing the firm's cash flow.

Nevertheless, even a concerted, regular effort to forecast revenue can lead to inaccuracies. Of all the elements that comprise the cash-flow projection, none is more difficult to pin down than cash inflow, the brunt of which is accounted for by sales. Still, any projections are better than none, and the manager who invests time in the process will have a better chance of keeping the firm liquid.

It's easy to project an overly optimistic sales or revenue forecast; after all, what kind of manager would you be if you weren't optimistic about forthcoming earnings? Preparing the cash projection is the wrong time, however, to be optimistic. It is the proper time to conservatively estimate sales and reflect some pessimism.

There are several ways to project revenue. Simply extrapolating past sales has some value—it gets you started. You don't want to fall into the trap of relying too heavily on past data; after all, what does the past have to do with current and forthcoming opportunities, especially in a dynamic business? Figure 1.3 cites some forecasting methods.

Probably the most effective way to forecast revenue is what we call "expected values." This method is particularly helpful if your revenues are derived in the form of contracts, but it can be adapted to fit many businesses. For simplicity of explanation, we will begin with a start-up firm that has no existing customers:

Suppose you recently started a laboratory supply company. For ease of illustration let's assume there are only three potential

---

Methods of Forecasting Revenue

Questionnaires. By surveying customers and prospective customers, some entrepreneurs are able to generate a rough 12-month revenue estimate.

Delphi Method. Using a group of experts—perhaps key members of your management staff, your board of directors, or an advisory board—to give their "best guess" as to what revenue will be. This method derives its name from the oracle of Delphi, who, according to the ancient Greeks, could foretell the future!

Regression Analysis. Plotting the change, hopefully upward, of your sales (the dependent variable) in relation to an independent variable, such as the number of bids made or product improvement, or to a combination of several independent variables.

Sales Force Estimates. Summing the individual projections of what each member of your sales staff thinks he or she can sell. This is an excellent way to establish a revenue forecast.

Forecasting Services. Using the industrial forecasts, by Standard Industrial Classification (SIC) codes, that are available from such firms as Predicasts and Dun & Bradstreet. However, a forecast for growth within an industry must be applied cautiously when forecasting revenue for an individual firm within the industry.

Other Industry Forecasts. Finding other forecasts within your industry. Such forecasts may be prepared by trade associations or research or advocacy groups.

Figure 1.3.

contracts on the horizon. You believe you have a reasonable chance of winning each of them. Contract A is with Taft Hospital and totals $75,000. Contract B is with Research Labs Unlimited and is for $50,000, and contract C is with the County Coroner and is for $40,000.

If you were an extreme optimist, your revenue forecast would be $165,000, reflecting the situation in which you won all three contracts. Since that outcome is unlikely, further analysis is needed to produce a revenue forecast that more closely reflects the dynamics of the marketplace.

Suppose that for Taft Hospital, you know of only two other firms that are bidding on the same contract and you have reason to believe your firm to be far superior to the competitors. On the second contract, with Research Labs Unlimited, you are not sure how many others are bidding on the job. However, you do know that there are at least four or five competitors, and you are only in the middle of the pack, having no particular competitive advantage.

On the third potential contract, with the County Coroner, you feel you are as good as "wired." Though your company is in a start-up phase, you have already visited them twice, they like you, and they have just about said, "The contract is yours." How does information on these three contracts affect your revenue forecast?

First, portray the current situation:

Organization	Size of Contract	Number of Competitors	How You Stand
Taft Hospital	$75,000	2	1st of 3?
Research Labs	$50,000	5	3rd of 6?
County Coroner	$40,000	0	1st of 1?

Table 1.2.

The contract with Taft Hospital will total $75,000, and whoever wins the contract will realize that full amount. The best information you have indicates that you are the leading candidate of three bidding for the job. Basing your evaluation on probability you might say that you have a 50 percent chance of winning the job. However, you will quickly see that assigning probabilities is a highly subjective art.

Maintaining a conservative posture, it makes sense to regard your probability of winning as 30 percent or less. You can never count on having accurate knowledge of the situation—things may change and it is best to be cautious when forecasting revenue. For the purposes of this example a 30-percent probability is reasonable. Multiplying 30 percent times $75,000, the face amount of the contract, yields an *expected value* for Taft Hospital of $22,500. More on this shortly.

On the Research Labs Unlimited contract, you are one of at least five firms bidding, and you have no apparent advantage. At first glance, you might presume that assigning a 20 percent chance of winning is appropriate. It's not, however, for the simple reason that there are too many unknowns in the situation. You may think you have a 10 or 15 percent chance of winning; however, assigning a five percent chance, or less, is more appropriate when there are many competitors and many unknowns.

On the Research Labs Unlimited contract the *expected value* of that particular contract is $50,000 times five percent, or a mere $2,500. Another way to look at the Research Labs contract is that, given the situation as portrayed above, if you made bids on 19 other contracts with similar situations, you could reasonably expect to win one (five percent or one in 20). A third way to regard the situation is that when you have many competitors, no competitive advantage, and no inside information, you could regard your probability of winning as nearly zero. Nevertheless, five percent remains appropriate for the situation as depicted.

On the County Coroner contract, now that you're seeing how *expected values* work, you may conclude that you have a 70 or 80 percent chance of winning what appears to be a contract that is "sewn up." Even under these conditions, it would be wiser to assign a probability of winning at 50 percent or less. You never know. On the third contract then, the expected value is $20,000 ($40,000 × 50 percent).

Summing the expected values for the three contracts yields a total expected value of contracts of $45,000. Surprise! No single contract equals $45,000, yet to the best of your knowledge thus far and ability to project, this figure represents the most appropriate revenue forecast for your firm.

This example has been simple in that you are a new company with no backlog, you are faced with three new contract possibilities, and you know the approximate number of competitors involved and where you stand among them. Also, the amounts of the contracts are fixed and they will all be awarded within a 12-month period.

This method of forecasting works the same whether you are facing 3 or 103 potential contracts or income opportunities, and can be staggered to reflect different starting dates and different payoff dates. The one factor that remains difficult to assess is the probability of winning. In many cases, you will have little or no information as to where you stand. There may be so many competitors that your probability might not exceed one percent.

MANY IRONS IN THE FIRE

The expected-value method of revenue forecasting underscores the basic need for many businesses to vastly increase revenue opportunities to improve cash flow. If your business has too few

Organization	Size of Contract	Probability of Winning	Expected Value of Contracts
Taft Hospital	$75,000	30%	$22,500
Research Labs	$50,000	5%	2,500
County Coroner	$40,000	50%	$20,000
			$45,000

Table 1.3.

possibilities in the pipeline, then you are relying too heavily on winning most of the few you bid on and are setting yourself up for a major cash trap. You must have many revenue possibilities in the pipeline at any one time, and try to get as much inside information as possible on where you stand in relation to competitors.

To return to our example, as time passes, and contract awards are made, your forecast changes. If you win the County Coroner contract for $40,000, the probability is no longer 50 percent, but becomes 100 percent. The expected value of that contract becomes the full $40,000. Your overall expected value of contracts jumps up to $65,000 (Table 1.4).

If the Research Labs contract goes to another firm, your expected value of winning becomes zero, and the expected value of that contract also becomes zero. Your total revenue forecast is then decreased by $2,500. Similarly, as you bid on other contracts and as new information is obtained, your forecast can be updated.

If you derive your revenues by ringing up customer sales one at a time at a cash register or from a shipping department, your revenue forecast can be constructed simply by projecting the number of customers to be served, or units to be moved, per hour, day, week, or larger unit of time and taking into account seasonal and cyclical factors.

Organization	Size of Contract	Probability of Winning	Expected Value of Contracts
Taft Hospital	$75,000	30%	$22,500
Research Labs	$50,000	5%	2,500
County Coroner	$40,000	100%	$40,000
			$65,000

Table 1.4.

MANAGING GROWTH AND FLUCTUATION

As any seasoned entrepreneur can tell you, low sales volume is not always at the root of liquidity problems. Rapid growth or, as we'll examine in Chapter 2, growth produced by fluctuating levels of business activity can create cash-flow problems by sending overhead expenses sky-high. Greater market penetration, a wider range of products, and additional customers can require huge outlays in cash in staff, office space, equipment, and raw materials.

As we'll discuss in Chapter 3, runaway inventory is another cause of cash-flow problems. Careful sales forecasts can also enable businesses to stock an adequate, but not a costly surplus of inventory. Don't take advantage of volume discounts if it means you'll be strapped for cash for months to come. Instead, determine the minimum amount of inventory you'll need to meet your projected sales for a specified period and place a "re-order" for that quantity when your stock drops to a safety level.

Work to develop or maintain an impeccable credit rating and make use of the many bank services available to you (see Chapter 5). A line-of-credit that costs you nothing until and unless you use it can be crucial in getting you thorough temporary cash shortages. Don't wait, though, until the wolf's at the door; apply for credit when business is good, or at least not horrible. Banks and everyone else are more likely to work with you if you approach them before you're in a cash trap.

Chapter 1: Hot Tips and Insights

✓ When you're continually strapped for cash, you lower the expectations and energy of even your most loyal staff and you dissipate the confidence others have in you.

✓ In a profitable business, over time, cash inflow should begin to outpace cash outflow and contribute to liquidity. As cash becomes available, the same diligence and frugality exhibited in lean times is not maintained, however, and as business expands the task of balancing inflows with unprecedented outlays to finance growth becomes taxing.

✔ The easiest way to stay abreast of your cash flow is to plot it manually or with any available spreadsheet program.

✔ It isn't difficult to produce a detailed cash-flow projection which ends up proving to be off by thousands if not tens of thousands of dollars. The assumptions made about the projected cash inflows and outflows are as important as the actual figures themselves.

✔ Once your cash-flow projection is up and operative, modifying it as time passes to maintain a 12-month projection need not take more than a couple of hours a week.

✔ One of the most effective ways to forecast revenue is called "expected values," which underscore the need for increased revenue opportunities. If you have too few possibilities in the pipeline, you're relying too heavily on winning most of the few you bid on and are setting yourself up for a major cash trap.

✔ Do not take advantage of volume discounts if it means you'll be strapped for cash for months to come. Instead, place the minimum "re-order" for when your stock drops to a safety level.

✔ Apply for credit when business is good, or at least not lousy.

2

PRUNING YOUR PAYROLL COSTS

Wages should be reckoned not by numbers of pounds or dollars, but in purchasing power of good things—of beauty as well as bread.

Philip Gibbs

You can't organize or operate your business without people, and it's likely that staff costs are one of your top two or three costs of doing business. This is particularly true if you are in a service-related business where payroll costs represent 60 to 70 percent or more of your operating costs. It is in people-intensive businesses that your creative management talents can help you do a more efficient job of operating your company and avoiding cash traps.

This chapter will help you creatively balance your staffing needs with the realities of your business needs. The first section offers innovative measures for taking some of the bite out of your weekly payroll costs. The second section of this chapter offers tips, ideas, and approaches that can help you manage and structure your core staffing and personnel strategy. The third section offers simple, but direct, hands-on tools to measure your productivity.

THINKING PERSONNEL, MAKING PAYROLL

Payroll costs, particularly in the entrepreneurial firm, are a bugaboo. Cash-flow and payroll concerns in many firms focus on the question, "Can I make payroll this week?" Simply: Do I have enough in the corporate checking account to cover the take-home payroll checks that have to be distributed tomorrow morning?

Let's see how to make your payroll dollars go further.

From 52 to 26, or 24 Pay Periods

First, convert from weekly pay periods to biweekly periods. The change from weekly payroll to biweekly (26 pay periods) or semimonthly (24 pay periods) does not reduce your payroll costs, but it offers a variety of other cost and administrative benefits. It lessens the payroll preparation process, reduces accounting overhead, and decreases the number of checks written per month.

It results in substantially higher interest earnings—you are now retaining funds for the equivalence of six months that otherwise would have been out of your control. Shifting salary payment cycles may also offer a one-shot bit of relief if your company's receivables pattern results in larger amounts of cash at certain times of the month.

Your firm may be faced with split check preparation schedules; the pay shift may need to be two-tiered. You may be able to pay office and supervisory personnel biweekly while retaining the weekly pay schedule for remaining employees.

Of course, you can't expect a shift in payroll disbursements to serve as a solution to cash-flow problems; it's simply a revolving, short-term aid. Also, your company pay practices usually need to be in tune with the payment patterns in your industry, region, and locale. You have to be sensitive to expectations and not risk losing valued employees because of a desire to shift payroll patterns. However, most employees accept the change by the third or fourth payment under the new plan.

Payroll Timing

Another aid, but not a cure, for a weak cash flow is to master the timing of payroll disbursements. When are the checks "normally" distributed in your company? Checks distributed after two o'clock on Friday cannot be processed or deducted from company accounts until the following week, often beyond Monday. Although many banks in your community are open late on Friday afternoons and maintain drive-up window service on Friday evenings and Saturday, these extended hours are for competitive reasons and customer convenience. Any check deposited after two o'clock on Friday or anytime on Saturday will not be entered into the bank's check processing system until the following Monday. In fact, most banks post-sign to notify customers of this fact and will date the customer's deposit receipt with the Monday date.

Try this yourself: Make a deposit after two o'clock on Friday afternoon and if your bank offers Saturday hours, make a Saturday deposit as well. Then look at the deposit receipt for the date. Later, double-check your monthly statement. You will probably find that your deposits were treated as if received on the following Monday and were processed then.

By dispensing payroll checks after two o'clock Friday afternoon, you get to "play the float" and continue to earn interest over the weekend, and probably for at least another day as well. Depending on your community and your bank's automated clearing activity, you can figure on a minimum of three days of interest, maybe four. Then consider that some payroll checks will not be deposited promptly, and some paychecks may be deposited at other banks, requiring an additional day or two to clear at your bank. Your firm will have four or possibly five days to earn interest on some portion of your payroll funds.

You can see how this can add up if you think that 24 or 26 times per year, you are earning three to five days interest on most if not all of your payroll expense. Hereafter, you may not want to write payroll checks on an account with the bank that most employees use, or the bank with the most branches, or the bank with the longest business hours. Interest earned on the float for any of the checks you write, including payroll checks, is extra cash.

For example, if you are paying 50 employees an average of $500 in take-home pay per week, a three-day float at seven percent interest earns you $2243.80 annually (nothing to sneer at):

$500 × 50 employees = $25,000 per week

$25,000 × 3 days × 7% (annual)/365 days = $43.15/week

$43.15 × 52 weeks = $2243.80

With 100 employees and higher take-home figures, the interest earned can exceed $5000, and so on.

Do some comparison shopping at local banks in your community every six months to see what types of programs they are offering business clients (more on banks in Chapter 6). Investigate any special programs geared to attract commercial clients, particularly their interest earning commercial savings accounts and commercial checking accounts.

Some local financial institutions want to encourage your business accounts and serve your employees. Remain alert to the fact that banks that offer automatic payroll deposits for employees—thereby potentially reducing employee transaction costs—could take away from your opportunity to earn interest on the float.

Be aware, however, that employee morale problems could erupt if you push the float too far. For instance, checks drawn on an out-of-state bank could mean that the employees could not "use" the money they earned for a week after they deposited their checks in their own checking accounts.

Availability of Funds for Withdrawal

Financial institutions today are required to make funds available according to strict deadlines based on the money instrument and the location of the paying bank. Here is a quick guide as to when one can withdraw funds based on deposits he or she has made based on Federal Reserve Regulation CC.

HOW LONG A BANK MAY HOLD DEPOSITED FUNDS

Available the next business day after a deposit:

- Cash
- U.S. Treasury checks
- State and local government checks (same state)

- Personal checks drawn on the same bank
- First $100 of any check
- Cashiers checks
- Certified checks
- Tellers checks
- Depository checks
- All wire transfers

Available no later than the second business day after a deposit:

- The remaining balance of all checks drawn on local institutions (within the same Federal Reserve Bank check–processing region).

Available no later than the fifth business day after a deposit:

- Remaining balances of all checks drawn on nonlocal financial institutions. Banks in Hawaii, Alaska, U.S. Virgin Islands, and Puerto Rico can take an extra business day to credit checks drawn on banking institutions not inside their geographic borders.
- The regulations do not apply to new accounts for the first 30 days.

If the above seems a little unreasonable, remember that if your employees are known by their respective banks, and have active accounts with them, then the regulations need only represent the worst case scenario for them. And though current regulations are supposed to prevail, not all banks comply with all aspects of the regulations at all times.

Pay Disbursement Impact

How and when you hand out paychecks on paydays can impact your business. What are the prevailing behavior patterns and rituals surrounding employee reception of paychecks that have become status quo in your firm? Some of these patterns may be so long-standing, that they're now regarded by employees as company-approved and taken as a benefit of working for your company.

If you disburse your paychecks Friday morning, which you now know costs you substantial interest earnings, for the next few paydays make some observations. Do people in your firm seem to be "away from their desk" or "out of the shop" on payday after paychecks are distributed? Check how many of your staff are taking long lunch hours or skipping out during midafternoon to undertake their weekly shopping, run to the bank, or attend to personal matters.

If your company payday is Thursday for the previous week, do you tend to have more absences on Friday? If you pay on Tuesday for the previous week, does the Tuesday lunch hour tend to be overly long? Do employees seem to be absent or ill more often on the day after payday? These absences add up week after week and nibble at overall productivity and effectiveness.

Leadership by example is crucial here. Is your staff simply emulating your habits? If you are inclined to take Friday afternoon off after you've distributed paychecks, the message you're sending is clear. If you take extra long lunch hours on payday to run personal errands, your staff will probably follow suit.

First in Leadership, Last in Pay, but Only for the Brave.   If you are the founder, president, or leader of your company, let it be known among the employees that you regard yourself as personally responsible for the products, quality, and management of the company and for any shortfalls within the organization. Make it known that you intend personally to earn less any week that performance levels drop and that you are not going to be happy in those circumstances. And then follow through by taking less.

Contrast this image of leadership to that which is regularly portrayed in the business press, where senior executives seemingly often receive ever-larger salaries and bonuses in the face of slumping performance and corporate layoffs.

This approach to leadership helps to drive home the importance of everyone's role in the company. It reinforces the importance of quality and competitive performance. It emphasizes that every paycheck must be earned, and that compensation and job security are dependent on the performance of the entire company.

This message is particularly applicable in small- and mid-sized companies, where individual effort can make a noticeable and immediate difference. In large corporations it is difficult to relate individual effort to the overall performance of the company and the company's ability to "make payroll." Figure 2.1 summarizes these ideas.

Getting the Most From Your Payroll Process

☐ Review paycheck disbursement time

☐ Check your employee paycheck deposit pattern

☐ Identify and monitor your payroll float

☐ Shop your local financial market for float potential

☐ Monitor employee behavior patterns on payday

☐ Evaluate your leadership signals

Figure 2.1.

TRIMMING PAYROLL COSTS

Often, business owners and managers respond to growth with an inclination to hire more people, usually full-time people. It may seem like the easiest way to meet daily needs. In hiring more full-time staff, your firm increases its fixed overhead and incurs greater costs through higher equipment use, increased telephone use, possibly the need for more space, more benefits, more health insurance, and more social security and unemployment taxes.

Think of your business as the process of converting human hours and human energy (your energy and that of your employees) into products, goods, and services. These products, goods, and services, in turn, become accounts receivable, and then come back to you in the form of checks. Many of those gross margin dollars go back out the door in the form of payroll checks. How well you organize, manage, and stimulate the people that you give the paychecks to, and how well you manage funds at your disposal, will determine your success.

A New View of Staffing

Significant savings on staffing is derived from two key areas: (1) increased employee productivity and (2) reducing the number of full-time staff and overhead through part-timers, work-for-hire employees, and outside professionals. Even in this era of corporate downsizing, in many organizations—including both big and small businesses and other institutions such as city, county, and state governments—employee staffing levels are still viewed as permanent.

Employment remains the same with relatively little regard to how much business or service activity is being produced. This is being stuck in a "comfort zone," which is a lose-lose situation. The company loses its competitiveness. Employees are unchallenged, underperforming, and probably looking for a way out.

A small data services business in northern Kentucky was being sunk by too many full-time staffers. The company was managed by its founder/president and employed an office manager/secretary, a sales and service manager, and six full-time staff employees responsible for most of the data entry. In addition, one or two part-time people were frequently used.

The problem was that the full-time staff, as small as it was, remained the same every month without regard for workload. Business fluctuated up or down by 15 to 35 percent each month. For almost two years the company was losing ground as its bills grew larger and further delinquent. The owner found it difficult to address the personnel staffing problem. He didn't really want to change the character of the daily operations.

"Just one" sizable, long-term contract (which always seemed to be on the horizon) could have cemented the need for at least six full-time data-entry staff. He was reluctant to admit that he was buying almost the same number of staff hours when business volume was $31,000 per month as when it was $48,000.

A major creditor and minority stock holder finally precipitated major staff changes and a corporate restructuring. The result was that the president and office manager became the *only* full-time employees. All other staff were converted into a pattern of part-time work (though for most this remained nearly full-time) keyed to the flow of business.

In sum, the company "bought" fewer staff hours and had a reduced payroll. The company also reduced its fixed overhead and began to realize positive margins on its work and to meet more of its bills on time. The reduction in full-time employment may be viewed as unfortunate for the employees; however, the survivability of the company and of their jobs was in doubt.

No One Wants To Be the Ax Man.   No one wants to be responsible for staff layoffs or a reduction in force. This is particularly true in smaller businesses where staff cutbacks impact on interpersonal relationships directly. However, unless a company can profitably manage its resources, including the purchase of staff time, it cannot offer secure employment to anyone.

Meeting Core Needs

The key to prudent staffing is meeting your core needs. Virtually every business has slack time and other periods when the demands on the company are greater. The challenge as an owner or manager is to structure the core staff to meet the core business demand. This requires thinking in terms of buying staff hours. Ultimately, you may have to buy staff hours to meet the demand based on time of day, week, or season.

Split shifts.   Companies of all types and sizes face difficult staffing tasks. The telephone companies, for example, have long known which hours of the day they receive the greatest number of requests for directory assistance; they therefore hire employees for split shifts to meet the demand. An information operator may work each day from 8:00 A.M. to 11:00 A.M. and from 3:00 P.M. to 7:00 P.M. Your local supermarket, fast-food operation, and local pizza delivery service meet their staffing needs in the same way. They schedule to meet the customer demand by the time of the day.

Review your business for demand patterns by day, week, month, and season. Are your staffing patterns and personnel strategy *demand linked* and *demand driven*? Or does your firm find itself looking for projects to "keep people busy" waiting for "something to come in"? The most successful firms in your industry and your most serious competition are those who proactively manage the high cost of personnel.

New Workforce Dynamics

Surprisingly, you may find qualified help who are readily willing to work odd schedules. The social and economic forces at work in our changing society are giving rise to new patterns of work, and these changes can be your ally in developing staffing strategy.

The new dynamics of work enable you to more easily meet the flexibility demand for staff assistance. Today more people will accept, and indeed seek, part-time work. Temporary services and related agencies who can supply you with all manner of skilled workers await your call. The dramatic growth of retirees, particularly relatively young, high-talent retirees spells opportunity for your business and avoidance of cash traps related to a heavy, fixed payroll.

The phenomenom of "restructuring," a euphemism for laying off people in larger firms, has altered many workers' willingness to exhibit life-long loyalty to a large corporation. A Conference Board study in the mid-1980s found that 12 million middle-level managers were systematically removed from the ranks of the corporate world either through layoffs, dead-end careers, or other pressures. Most opted for careers within existing small businesses or started their own ventures. More and more excorporate staff are willing to work as independent consultants.

Consultants, in particular, can be a valuable source of short-term expertise. They do not require permanent office space or permanent secretarial support and they do not notably increase overhead costs such as telephones, copiers, and vacation pay. These costs are shifted to the consultants, who tend to earn higher wages per hour, but the wages are almost always job-specific costs that can be negotiated and evaluated as each specific assignment is made.

The Home-Business Boom

The explosive growth in home-based businesses and home-based workers and consultants offers a nearly inexhaustible supply of local talent. In many ways, we're about to witness the most profound workforce change since the post–World War II period. The statistics are irrefutable; the growth in the number of home-based businesses is a global phenomenon. Surveys indicate that more than 40,000,000 Americans now perform some or all of their work out of their homes. This figure could rise by another 10,000,000 by 1995.

In addition, working women, minorities, the handicapped, and immigrants increasingly are seeking to achieve business success outside of the limited corporate structure. The high divorce rate in society also has prompted many working parents, who need to care for or wish to stay in greater contact with their children, to seek home-based business alternatives.

The unprecedented growth of telecommuting means that you need not always provide permanent office space for full-time employees. Faxes, phones, beepers, modems, personal copiers, E-mail, answering services, cellular phones, and the like enable you to stay in close contact with the telecommuter.

By determining what range of activity can be met by part-time or nontraditional employees, your business can be more competitive and more profitable. Yes, new thinking and innovative work arrangements will be necessary to take advantage of the opportunities. At the same time, increasingly, businesses have no choice but to adapt.

Strategies for Identifying Supplemental Staff Sources

The key to building the supplemental staff is recognizing the need to continually cultivate resource contacts and develop networks of additional potential "employees" who as either consultants or subcontractors can expand the productive capacities of your firm.

An effective way to identify individuals and consultants who may be available and interested in supplementing your staff is to advertise for them. You can do this in the same way you would to find permanent employees. Place blind advertisements (not identifying your firm) in local newspapers seeking potential supplemental or full-time staff. You may be surprised, even overwhelmed, by the number of *qualified* applicants you identify.

If you need only specific skills for specific tasks, be fair and accurate in composing your classified advertisement.

If you want to identify a pool of additional part-time staff with the possibility of some full-time work, indicate the opportunity for both full- and part-time staff.

If you are in need of supplemental staff for certain hours or can offer flextime work, emphasize the hours as a special feature. If you are located in a small town and you don't think there are enough skilled people in your immediate community, try the newspaper in the next largest community.

Additional sources for part-time staff or consultants include the following: local community colleges or universities (students and faculty), local business groups and service organizations, existing core or supplemental staff employees, community or weekly newspapers, and other people within your field.

You may recruit supplemental staff for one type of work and then decide to cross-train the person to handle several different types of tasks. Business students eager for experience while attending the local community college or university would fall into this category. A quality control or inventory specialist may also make a good accounts payable or receivables clerk. If you are looking for industry-specific skills or trade experience, you may be able to hire someone who has retired from a competitor's firm.

The only limiting factors in building a supplemental staff are your imagination and your own willingness to seek them out.

Investing in Your Core Staff

Flexible staffing enables your company to help its full-time permanent staff become more responsible and more productive. You can invest in more training and equipment to make your core employees more productive and more valuable and spend far less overall than you would if you attempted a lesser investment spread across a larger staff.

You will be able to expand core staff responsibilities to include management of supplemental staff. The result will be greater control over lower "fixed" payroll costs, but perhaps the most important benefit of core staffing strategy is that it helps keep you out of the comfort-zone trap.

PERSONNEL PRODUCTIVITY RATIO

How can you simply but clearly determine productivity in your own company? The ideal productivity measure is to gauge personnel efficiency to production over short time periods. An example would be to determine how many employee hours were used to work a specific lunchtime shift at a fast-food outlet and how many lunches were served. When you don't sell easily divisible units of a product directly to end-users, other ways of gauging productivity are called for.

We suggest developing your own broad increments of measure. We'll discuss two very broad measures here. The first is the *Payroll Cost-to-Sales ratio*, a measure which answers the question, "What did it cost the company in salary, wages, and commissions to generate its total gross sales?"

Payroll Cost-to-Sales Ratio

This first measure is the easiest to compute because the company sales figures and payroll are generally available. Most organizations, even smaller businesses, have this broad data available by month, quarter, and year. You can use this measure to judge seasonal changes in both sales and staff costs. It focuses one's attention on how many payroll dollars your firm spent and staff hours it bought, and how much this effort produced in sales.

Payroll costs are used as a convenient substitute for actual work hours because payroll figures are usually the most readily available. If your firm has records that also provide work hours or workdays, these figures can be used to reflect the actual amount of work hours "purchased" to produce and support the firm's sales.

As easy as this broad measure is to compute, often business

owners and managers are caught up in daily tasks and fail to take even this broad look at operations. Two characteristics, unique to each company, should be taken into account at this broad level. The first is lead time. Take care to match staffing costs to revenue in a comparable time period. If your business produces, ships, and invoices in a relatively short time period there is little difficulty. If you incur longer "lead times" between the work effort and when sales occur, you have to adjust your analysis.

The second characteristic is applicability. If your company has more than one division or if the nature of the work differs from one division to another, payroll costs to sales may not be as useful in charting productivity. In the case where your firm has either more than one division or undertakes different types of activity that require different types of employees, the evaluations should remain separated by company divisions.

In any case, the payroll cost-to-sales ratio is most useful in comparing business activity over broad periods of time. Table 2.1 demonstrates how a broad and reasonably quick evaluation may be very useful.

From this quick analysis, it is clear that the growth in sales from Year 1 to Year 2 was accompanied by a greater increase in payroll costs over that of sales. For each dollar of additional sales, payroll costs increased during Year 2 over the ratio in Year 1. This does not necessarily mean the company did anything wrong, rather that it incurred proportionally greater payroll costs to achieve the higher level of sales in Year 2.

If the company does not have a clear understanding why it

Payroll Cost-to-Sales Ratio

	Year 1	Year 2	Year 3
Gross Sales	$400,000	$505,000	$630,000
Payroll Costs	$90,000	$138,000	$157,000
Ratio	22.5%	27.3%	24.9%

Table 2.1.

incurred higher payroll costs, then it could find itself at risk for a protracted period of lower earnings or losses—the ultimate cash trap.

In the third year, payroll costs as a percent of sales were lower. This observation would aid in evaluating prices and products, perhaps new equipment, new business, and the number and types of staff hours the company buys.

Payroll Cost-to-Gross Margin Ratio

This ratio is a refinement of ratio discussed above. It factors out what you purchase from others, the "cost of goods sold" category. In its simplest terms, you begin with your gross sales figures and subtract the cost of goods sold. This resulting figure is your gross margin. It is the amount of money you have available to pay salaries, rent, utilities, advertising, delivery costs, and all other operating expenses.

With this ratio you can gain an understanding of your total payroll costs, including all indirect costs such as health insurance, social security taxes, workers' compensation, and unemployment tax, as compared to the gross margin dollars you have earned to meet all your operating expenses. Depending on your line of business, it may be useful to measure how your firm compares from one season to the next, or from one year to the next.

If you usually achieve a ratio of 50 percent and business slows or demand for your products or services becomes weaker, you may find that for several weeks or a month your payroll costs will edge up toward 60 percent of gross margin. This, of course, is a key indicator that you are buying more staff hours with fewer gross margin dollars. Understandably, your cash flow will be squeezed and you may be headed for a serious cash trap.

When sales increase, and the gross margin increases, and payroll costs fall, in basic terms you will have increased your personnel productivity. The odds are that your cash flow will also improve dramatically.

In Table 2.2, payroll costs are increasing as a percentage of the gross margin, the company's disposable dollars. From Year 1 to

Payroll Cost to Gross Margin

	Year 1	Year 2	Year 3
Gross Sales	$450,000	$570,000	$650,000
Cost of Goods Sold	300,000	380,000	420,000
Gross Margin	150,000	190,000	230,000
Staff & related	90,000	120,000	150,000
Ratio	60.0%	63.2%	65.2%

Table 2.2.

Year 3, payroll and related costs increased from 60.0 percent to 65.2 percent as compared to the gross margin. Payroll costs also increased as a percentage of gross sales from 20 percent to 23.1 percent.

The company in the example may have undertaken more work that was manpower intensive; it may have "bought" more management staff in expectations of future growth; it may have increased its salaries without raising prices; or it may have incurred more overtime expense. Again, a crude measure is all that's necessary to stimulate further investigation of the root causes.

The specific figures for your business will vary depending on your type of business, years in business, market(s) served, technology employed, number of employees, and a host of other factors. So it makes sense to employ the financial sources cited on page 20, in Chapter 1. Regardless of your type of business, however, it's likely that payroll costs will always account for a large, if not the largest slice of your expenses. With that in mind, vigorously pursue any measure that enables you to conserve dollars while still performing up to par.

Chapter 2: Hot Tips and Insights

✓ Staff costs are likely one of your top two or three costs of doing business particularly if you are in a service-related

business where payroll costs represent 60 to 70 percent or
more of your operating costs.

✓ Particularly in people-intensive businesses, your creative
management talents can help you do a more efficient job
of operating your company and avoiding cash traps.

✓ Convert from weekly pay periods to biweekly periods,
which offers a variety of cost and administrative benefits,
such as reducing the payroll preparation process, accounting overhead, and the number of checks written per month.

✓ Distribute payroll checks after 2:00 P.M on Friday, since
the checks cannot be processed or deducted from company
accounts until the following week, often beyond Monday.

✓ You may choose not to write payroll checks on an account
with the bank that most employees use, or the bank with
the most branches, or with the longest business hours.
Interest earned on the float for any of the checks you write,
including payroll checks, is extra cash.

✓ When you pay employee benefits for your staff, generally
you can deduct their wages and their benefits. Your employees are able to have more discretion over their wages
since they come in purer form—benefits need not be paid
for by employees with before-tax dollars. The upshot is
that you can offer somewhat lower wages and both you
and your employees actually come out ahead.

✓ How and when you hand out paychecks on paydays does
impact your business, and your staff is likely to emulate
your behavior around pay time.

✓ Significant savings on staffing can be derived from two key
areas: increased employee productivity and reducing the
number of full-time staff and overhead through part-timers, work-for-hire employees, and outside professionals.

✓ Review your business for demand patterns by day, week,
month, and season. Are your staffing patterns and personnel strategy *demand linked* and *demand driven*? Or does
your firm look for projects to "keep people busy" while
waiting for "something to come in"?

✓ The most successful firms in your industry and your most serious competition are those who proactively manage the high cost of personnel. Your core staff can be far smaller than your flexible staff. Think in terms of buying staff hours. You may have to buy staff hours to meet the demand based on time of day, week, or season, but this approach will be less costly than retaining an unnecessarily large permanent staff.

✓ Today you can more easily find qualified help who are willing to work odd schedules. Social and economic forces are giving rise to new patterns of work, and these changes can be your ally in developing staffing strategy.

✓ With telecommuting you need not provide permanent office space for even full-time employees. Faxes, phones, beepers, modems, personal copiers, E-mail, answering services, and cellular phones enable you to stay in close contact with the telecommuter.

✓ Using flexible staffing, you can help your reduced full-time permanent staff become more responsible and more productive by offering them more training and equipment.

3

PRUDENT PURCHASING

Bring your desires down to your present means.
Increase them only when your increased means
permit.

Aristotle

The key to prudent purchasing is to become proactive in
spending your money. If you take command of your purchasing
program, you can develop an opportunistic outlook that will lead
to substantial savings when buying equipment and supplies. This
chapter offers new ideas for prudent purchasing and different
ways to view the cost, value, and control of your assets.

Purchasing means different things to people in different businesses. For many in service businesses purchasing may simply
mean buying office supplies from the local office supply store or
arranging for the purchase or lease of another copier. It also may
mean having the responsibility to establish and fully equip a new
branch location with everything from paper clips and chairs to
office and manufacturing or technical equipment.

In small- to medium-sized organizations, purchasing may be
an ancillary responsibility delegated to a secretary or office manager. Usually, the importance of purchasing activities and the
human resources devoted to it depend on the nature of the company and the amount and nature of purchasing activity.

THE BIGGEST CASH TRAP

When you remain liquid, you can buy things for less money. As we'll explore, suppliers are more inclined to do business with and offer more favorable terms to a firm or individual that pays promptly. Banks are willing to give lower interest rates to customers who maintain a strong cash position.

How you make your purchases and control your inventory impacts your liquidity and may be your company's single largest cash trap. Outside of payroll costs, the purchase of goods or raw materials for resale (cost of goods sold, "COGS") is usually the greatest single cost of operating the business. The inventories that COGS comprise are usually the company's single largest asset.

For each dollar of sales generated in a retail business, the costs of goods ranges from 70 to 74 percent of sales. For wholesale businesses, the costs of goods sold is closer to 75 percent. For a small, incorporated manufacturing concern, the costs of goods sold can average anywhere between 60 to 75 percent of total sales. From the remaining gross margin of 25 to 40 percent, all compensation, rents, repairs, fixed expenses of doing business, advertising, interest, taxes, and employee benefits must be covered.

It stands to reason that how and what you buy can make or break your cash flow and your business.

Identify Multiple Sources of Supply.   If your business involves the resale of some type of durable or nondurable goods, and your sources of supply are concentrated among two or three distributors, you are in a somewhat precarious position. If one of these suppliers can no longer deliver, or can no longer meet your need, your costs may skyrocket as you turn to alternative, quick-fix solutions. You never want to be among the long list of businesses that relied on one main source of supply, experienced a supply cutoff (or sharp increase in price), and found themselves with no alternative.

It is prudent purchasing strategy to develop multiple sources of supply. If you run a small business and your buying power is not significant, you have to work that much harder to achieve advantages in price and terms. Otherwise, your costs of goods sold, all other things being equal, may continually be higher than those of other larger competitors.

Keys to Your Success. If your business requires large inventories, purchasing strategy may be the key to the success of your business. Poorly managed purchasing (and inventory) can put any firm in jeopardy. Attend any corporate bankruptcy liquidation and you can hear participants wonder aloud how and why the defunct company "accumulated all this 'stuff.' "

Continually seek purchasing intelligence. Are there associations in your field which sponsor group purchasing programs? (The addresses of two key association directories are provided on page 107 in Chapter 6.) Are there merchants nearby who are willing to make combined purchases with you? Have you investigated any buying groups that may represent your industry and who could potentially save you tens of thousands of dollars each month? If not, check out the *Directory of Hard Lines Distribution* and *Who's Who, Wholesaler Groups*, both published by Chilton Books, 1 Chilton Way, Radnor, PA 19089.

PURCHASING IS NEGOTIATING

Contrary to conventional wisdom, there are many instances in which you do not want to be your supplier's favorite customer. The mind-set of the proactive purchaser is be a hunter, and not the hunted—view all purchases as negotiable. Price, quantity, and delivery are variables, and are not set in concrete. Circumstances change as well. Your suppliers regularly encounter customers who cancel orders, refuse delivery, or fail to make payment for COD deliveries. Other customers go bankrupt.

Previously "sold out" goods can suddenly become available, perhaps at distressed prices, for anyone who can move quickly to take advantage of the situation. Every industry has its share of individuals and companies who have earned the reputation for making shrewd and uncanny purchases. This is not a random phenomenon. The leadership and character of such a company is one that fosters and seeks favorable purchasing opportunities and then negotiates to make them even more favorable. These buyers discipline themselves to be selective, to wait, to say "no," knowing that today's seemingly bargain price for goods may be exorbitant compared with tomorrow's. Your goal is to be known as the buyer who hunts for values.

The best purchaser/negotiators seek out situations in which they can hone their skills. They use both calculated and spontaneous approaches to deal-making, knowing that frequently there is no time to prepare for outstanding, but fleeting, purchasing opportunities.

Pass Your Skills on to Others. If you run a small firm and are adept at purchasing, pass along this skill to your staff. Encourage the development of your staff's negotiating skills and allow them to gain experience. When your company is consciously predisposed to proactive purchasing policies, the cost of your purchases suddenly begins to drop. Whether it's a carton of envelopes, a dozen stacking trays, or enough packing crates to last until next June, deals start showing up.

Passing on your purchasing skills is particularly important in a family business if your sons and daughters work for you. Give them room to fail, because their success can easily outweigh the costs of a few bad buys.

Remember that effective purchasing and negotiating has less to do with price and quantity issues and more to do with human insight, personal interaction, and listening skills. Your supplier not only wants to sell his goods or services, but needs to. Frequently, we don't make vendors work for our business; we allow ourselves to be taken for granted. We fail to make suppliers "sell us." In many, many instances more favorable terms than those posted await. The key is to ask for them—a no-lose proposition.

The Purchasing-Negotiating Matrix

The Purchasing-Negotiating Matrix shown in Figure 3.1 is designed to help you characterize and assess the types of proactive choices you have when contemplating purchases. It reveals how price, quantity, type, delivery, warranties, payment, and other terms can be parlayed to your advantage when negotiating.

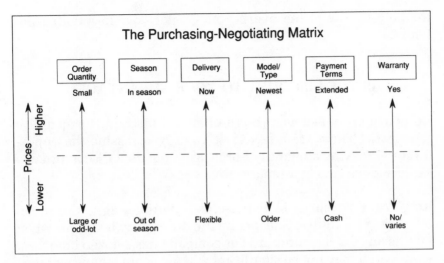

Figure 3.1.

For example, if you want a small quantity of the latest, hottest item in season right now, with credit terms and full warranty, expect to pay "full retail." If you are willing to pay in cash for an odd lot of off-season goods—you guessed it, a favorable deal for you is probable. The scale is relative and subjective, but it works like a dream in actual negotiations.

You may want to photocopy and post this matrix for quick referral. The matrix can also be used by sales and purchasing managers as a tool for staff development.

One particularly shrewd buyer routinely asks his suppliers, "What is your slowest sales month, and what kind of terms will you offer if I place a large order on the first of that month?" Not surprisingly, he has garnered some real sweetheart deals that make both parties happy.

If your purchase patterns consistently run across the top elements of the matrix, you're leaving yourself little room to negotiate and will rarely get good deals. You are paying premium prices for terms you may not need. Hereafter, whenever you negotiate a purchase, consider each of the matrix variables and its importance for the deal in question.

Depending on the nature of your business and purchasing need, and the specifics of the item(s) sought, the best buys of your career await. The more often you can accept terms along the bottom row of the matrix, the greater your negotiating potential.

IS THE DISCOUNT TO *YOUR* ADVANTAGE?

Do you jump whenever you're offered a discount for quantity purchases? There are a few basic rules to assessing the opportunity of making a quantity purchase to obtain a discount. Let's explore them one at a time:

Keep Your Purchase in Perspective. Purchasing is the trade-off of cash for things. Cheaper by the dozen may be useful when purchasing fax machines if your company has a dozen branches. However, it may not be significant when you are buying staplers. Every dollar you spend for, say, office equipment is a dollar you don't have as liquid cash to pay rent, make payroll, or purchase inventory. A quantity discount for items you don't need to be holding is no bargain.

Ask the DO and WHEN Questions. Anytime you're confronted with a quantity discount ask yourself two questions:

DO I really need this much?

WHEN can I reasonably expect to use or sell this?

Many opportunities are offered to you because the supplier does not want to be stuck with old or slow-moving inventory. Even if you have the storage space for an out-of-season item, evaluate your ability to use or resell the product, and consider the time and space required.

If you still want to make the buy, you don't have to take the first offer. Counter with a lower price to test the supplier's desire to move the goods. Too many quantity purchase decisions are made to satiate a buyer's thirst for a deal—for lower per-unit prices.

Step back a moment when you find yourself on the receiving end of a sales presentation or promotion geared to accelerate decision making—the old "buy it now, so I can lock it in for you pitch." Keep asking yourself the DO and WHEN questions. It's often true that the easiest person to sell to is a salesman, so if your background is sales, keep that in mind when it comes to purchasing.

Recognize What Drives Your Purchasing Decisions. Prudent purchasers consciously initiate purchasing decisions as part of a proactive strategy. Quantity purchase discounts are structured to provide the purchaser an incentive to do the seller a big favor, namely, "buy a lot of my goods." So long as you remain clear as to why you're buying, quantity purchases at a discount make sense. However, never forget, that purchasing converts cash, the most liquid asset, to inventory, a nonliquid asset, and potentially large cash traps. Few things hurt a business more than cash resources locked up in dead inventory worth perhaps only a fraction of its cost.

In today's technology-driven economy, low unit prices for large quantity orders work well only when you can use or resell the purchased goods in a reasonable period of time. Many items are sold at bargain prices just before the next model is ready.

If You've Got the Dough. After you've made a purchase, often you have the opportunity to take a prompt payment discount, though they often appear in very tiny print. If you have the cash, take them; forget them if you don't.

The terms may appear as "2/10 net 30" or may be printed in a date-like form like "2/10/30." This means the selling firm is offering you a two percent discount if you pay the invoice within 10 days. If you do not take the discount, the full invoice amount is due in 30 days.

A 2/10-net-30 discount on a $100 dollar purchase, taken 12 times each year means that you were able to save $24 off your purchases of $1200, which is still only two percent. Hundreds of finance books and thousands of articles will tell you it's like getting an exorbitant loan because you were alleviated of two percent of your burden over twelve 20-day time periods. The champions of this school of finance maintain that a 20-day interest rate of two percent taken 12 times compounds to more than 36 percent when annualized. The problem is that you're not building interest; you're reducing a recurring cost. No matter how you slice it, even *if you compound the $2 you save each month, at the end of a year, you still have saved only $36 or $37 for $1200 worth of purchases.*

Moreover, we could launch an extended discussion on the opportunity cost of departing with $98 20 days earlier than you had to 20 times a year. While $37 may be worth saving, it is not worth all that excitement.

THE ANATOMY OF COMMERCIAL DISCOUNTS

In business, discounts generally fall into a couple of categories:

Trade Discounts. This is a percentage off the manufacturer's, distributor's, or dealer's "list price." The amount of discount depends on the nature of the seller-buyer relationship with the market channel, and it takes into account transportation, advertising, warehousing, and local market servicing.

Trade discounts tend to be product-line or industry related and may involve one-, two-, or three-tier discounting. A two-step trade discount is spoken of as "30 and 10" or "30 and 15" The discounts are calculated in sequence, as the "30 and 15." example in Table 3.1 illustrates.

A 30 percent first-level discount and a 15 percent second-level discount may seem like "about 45 percent off," but it's really only 40.5 percent off. A three-step discount might be "25, 10, and 10%," as shown in Table 3.2.

Two Step Discount		
List price	$	100.00
First Discount, 30%	−	30.00
Gross Price	$	70.00
Second Discount, 15%	−	10.50
Discounted Price	$	59.50

Table 3.1.

Three Step Discount

List Price	$1,000.00
First Discount, 25%	− 250.00
Gross Price	$ 750.00
Second Discount, 10%	− 75.00
Wholesaler's Price	$ 675.00
Third Discount, 10%	− 67.50
Discounted price	$ 607.50

Table 3.2.

In this example, the three-step discount may reflect the purchase cost to the regional wholesaler-distributor set by manufacturer at $607.50. When the regional wholesaler sells the product to a local distributor or dealer, the transaction price may be $675. The local dealer could, in turn, sell the item to a commercial account or end-user for $750 to reflect a 25 percent discount off list price, or the dealer could sell it for any amount up to $1,000. The actual discount for a "25, 10, 10" discount pattern is less than 40 percent overall.

Cash Discounts. Almost everyone is familiar with cash discounts or so-called early or prompt-pay discounts. With many prompt-pay discounts if you are at, or within a day or two of cut-off date, you can call the vendor and, given that you have a record of prompt payments, have them extend the discount time slightly.

Anytime you are requested to offer *cash with the order*, you have negotiating strength on your side and can seek additional price concessions. There are two sides to every transaction. If you are asked to provide cash with an order, you are supporting another firm's cash flow and are taking a major risk. The vendor may not deliver the right product or may not get to the right location on time.

You are also at risk because vendors do go out of business—

there is nothing like calling a company whom you have paid in advance and finding their telephone disconnected! For any cash-with-order transaction, first judge the reliability and financial soundness of the supplier, and second, evaluate the time frame for both the production and delivery of the product.

Advance Partial Payments. Many businesses, particularly smaller businesses, seek partial payments or deposits in advance for certain types of work. You may be on either side of this transaction. If a supplier needs special items not regularly in his inventory, or if the job you want done requires special sub-contractors or extra labor, your supplier may ask for a deposit to cover payroll.

If you are asked for partial payment in advance, again, seek a lower price. It is reasonable to offer partial payment in advance, but avoid letting the supplier "get too far ahead" of you in cash versus product value or labor, unless you are otherwise reasonably secure. Advance partial payment or deposit with order may not present as strong a negotiating position as cash with order, but it is still a strong position in which to develop favorable terms.

Cash for Shipment. You may be asked to do business on a cash-for-shipment basis, perhaps because of delinquency in paying past invoices. If you are asked for cash for shipment, first consider:

- Have you previously paid your bills promptly?
- Is the purchase for a standardized, in-stock item?
- Are you a regular customer?

If your previous invoices with the supplier have been paid in a timely manner, ask for an open account or line-of-credit account with 30-day terms and discounts for prompt payment or other discounts.

Many requests of cash for shipment are a result of companies not having business experience with the buyer. They simply do not wish to take open, 30-day account receivable risks and hence request cash up front. If you are faced with cash-for-shipment requests, focus your negotiations around two issues—price discounts and delivery or freight allowances.

Your goal is to obtain some benefit that has a cost/price impact on the transaction. If the delivery or transportation cost is included or is very low relative to the item and transaction, focus your attention on the price discount.

If the product is readily available from many suppliers and they all use their own vehicles, negotiating lower freight allowances is useless. However, almost every business acquires goods for which the supplier's transportation costs are either imbedded in the price or separately billed. You can aid your negotiation by looking for ways to help the seller meet your reduced price goals by asking for either freight allowances or possibly credits towards additional purchases. This approach gives both parties something to barter over.

Remember, you have to ask for discounts and allow yourself to be courted as a customer. The person you are dealing with may not have authority to go below a certain price level, but he or she may be able to offer other concessions.

Cash on Delivery.   Usually, but not necessarily, firms "on COD," or cash on delivery, have previously failed to pay invoices promptly. If your account is *now* current with a supplier who has placed your firm on COD, do not be bashful: go back and ask for a COD discount. You have nothing to lose and only a discount to gain.

If the supplier requires COD because your firm is a new account and has no history or credit standing with the supplier, seek discounts for COD status. The supplier does not have to carry an account receivable and gains a cash-for-shipment transaction. A side benefit to you of COD transactions is the short-term float of the funds. The carrier who delivers the product and takes the check incurs an administrative and processing activity, and that works in your favor.

PAYING IT SLOW

There are times when delaying payment makes sense, or is non-negotiable, but as a cash-flow strategy it's often lame; it neither increases revenue, profitability, loyalty, or friendship among your suppliers or creditors. It's a holdover strategy from the era when people were willing to tolerate "the check is in the mail" type of excuses. Worse, it's a self-deceiving delaying tactic; holding checks never eradicates the root causes of why you have to delay payment in the first place.

Appropriate Delay of Payments.   When does it make sense to pay slow? Whenever you pay by credit cards, use the 25-day grace period during which you incur no interest charges. Pay the balance in full by the due date, and you've not only had an extra month or so of "cash" in your pocket, you've also received an interest-free loan.

If you receive a bill from a creditor on the 28th of April, and it's not due until the 28th of May, unless you want to earn any early payment discount, send your check out on May 23. Chapter 8 discusses how to set up a simple filing system so you can send out checks just before they're due, but always on time. Also, several software programs, discussed in Chapter 8, will remind you when bills are due.

When you are desperate or have few options, pay bills in order according to their penalties. Pay off credit cards with exorbitant 14 to 18 percent annual charges first. Many suppliers are willing to negotiate payment arrangements. Vendors may be willing to "give" a little if it means keeping a steady, bill-paying customer on the books or making a big sale.

If you've been a collection problem for your suppliers, all is not lost. First, stop playing games with your payments. "The check is in the mail" is an irritating, overly used stall. If you need to stall, be up front with it. It's better to be forthright and late than conniving and late.

To reestablish a good credit rating, enclose a personal, detailed letter to each supplier or creditor with the next payment due, explaining the reasons for slow payment in the past, and offering a brief synopsis of present operations. Thank the supplier for exhibiting patience (and support, if applicable) with the assurance that every effort is being made and will continue to be made towards the development of a solid working relationship.

When in doubt, follow the path of integrity. In the short run, you may take some knocks. In the long run, you'll always come out ahead. With suppliers, if your relationship has been honest, they can become valuable sources of short-term financing, via the extension of trade credit.

NEVER FALL IN LOVE WITH YOUR INVENTORY

Inventory is the flip side of purchasing. Items purchased for business are either to be used, consumed, transformed, or resold. Often something happens that interrupts inventory turnover, and the items "take up residence in the firm," becoming like comfortable old shoes, not attracting much attention or causing any trouble. However, they are cash traps—when in doubt, move it out!

Inventory that turns over far slower than the norms for your industry or line of business, or that becomes outdated, for whatever reason, is best cleared out. These are the large, seemingly harmless, slowly growing white elephants that tie up dollars and don't do much else. They grow old and stale, or are surpassed by the next, more attractive model, or accumulate a comfortable layer of dust. Employees tend to ignore them. This is the genesis of dead and useless inventory.

Today, virtually all computer dealers have old monitors, software, and accessories that they thought would sell. They failed to react to either price, market trends, or the anticipation of new models. Your goal is to constantly seek creative ways to dispose of what is not moving. Are there salvage stores, jobbers, remainder sellers, and other vendors who'll pay lump, though small, sums to take them off your hands? If so, your best move may be to get what you can when you can.

Keeping inventory moving in any line of business, in fact, can be a challenge. If it doesn't move in the normal course of business, you have to initiate action to move it out:

- It is better to sell at a lower margin than you'd like than to not make a profit at all.
- It is better to sell at cost than to never sell at all.
- It is better to sell at a loss than to have it sold by the bankruptcy trustee.

And, it is better to give to charity and take a tax deduction than to get nothing for it. Inventory *worth keeping*, but not worth storing on expensive leased property can be less expensively housed in leased warehouse space or in increasingly available public warehousing on a month-to-month or season-to-season basis. Most facilities will accommodate individual user needs regarding storage and distribution.

NEW ISN'T NECESSARILY BETTER

For some strange reason, many buyers are fixated on purchasing only new equipment whenever there is a need. Printers want the newest label presses and restaurant owners want sparkling new meat lockers and bread slicers.

If equipment is not visible to customers and need not otherwise represent the latest model, why not save a couple thousand on secondhand goods? A restaurant patron cares only what the food tastes like, not whether the meat locker looks new. Customers that come into your print shop won't know if the equipment is the latest, even if they see it.

Glance through the classified sections of your industry's journals and magazines and you'll see that the "equipment for sale" section is usually substantial. Why? One reason is that many businesses fail (they probably bought all their equipment brand new at top dollar) and a lot of equipment is being sold at liquidation prices (see "Develop a New Hobby—Attend Bankruptcy Auctions" later in this chapter). Another reason is that many businesses have been successful and are simply ready to buy equipment with greater capabilities.

Most of the equipment listed is in good working order and costs 50 percent or less of the latest models. In every major city one can find business equipment brokers who buy, sell, and lease new and used business and office equipment in your industry.

It also pays to explore equipment leases. This is a great way to make use of vital equipment without tying up dollars in its purchase. The less you have paid up front to equip your facilities, the more liquid you can remain both to create a safety buffer for the firm and to take advantage of other opportunities as they arise. More cash under your control means that you are in a better position to stay flexible as growth, revenue, and product patterns emerge.

SUPERSTORES SPELL COMMODITY SAVINGS

Unless you've been in Antarctica, you're probably already aware of the emergence of the superstores for attractive prices for office supplies and computer-related equipment. Behemoths such as the Price Club, Staples, Micro Center, Comp U.S.A., and others are carving a wide swath through urban and suburban America.

The Soft Warehouse, for example, is a super retailer that is making an immediate and lucrative splash catering to the PC users and peripherals market. Located in Atlanta, Chicago, Dallas, Denver, Detroit, Houston, Los Angeles, Miami, Palo Alto, Philadelphia, San Diego, and Washington, the chain offers 30 percent or more off retail prices on a large selection of micro computers, software, peripherals, computer systems, accessories, business machines, furniture, and supplies.

The typical store ranges anywhere from 17,000 to 35,000 square feet and stocks more than 5000 computer-related products, including a wide assortment of brand name PC-compatibles, printers, monitors, and related hardware, lap tops, disks, papers, supplies, storage equipment, and communication devices, as well as 2000 different software packages. To maintain the image of a price-conscious vendor, many of the products offered by the Soft Warehouse remain on pallets or in neat stacks on the floor unpacked, in their original boxes.

To be sure, the Comp U.S.A. *does not* offer prices competitive with those of direct mail advertising in the back of trade magazines. However, the giant store enables you to touch and talk before you buy. This type of store also offers a place to return your purchases as well.

A Member, Not Just a Customer.   At Staples, which advertises itself as the office superstore, free memberships are offered that entitle you to the "member price" on advertised specials. The member prices are a good deal, but they are even a better deal for Staples. The cards are bar-coded, and the clerk scans them, along with your purchases, at the checkout. This gives Staples daily sales data on their most frequent customers.

DEVELOP A NEW HOBBY—ATTEND BANKRUPTCY AUCTIONS

Attending a bankruptcy auction offers the opportunity to do some prudent purchasing of items usable in your business. Conversely, it will help you appreciate the cash trap that many of your inventory items really represent. How do you find these auctions? Many auctions, are advertised in the classified sections of newspapers.

Many auctioneers also advertise in the yellow pages and can help you get on auction mailing lists. Private auctions, estate sales, bankruptcy and liquidation sales, computer "expos" (which often feature a considerable number of second-hand goods), small business fairs, and other types of sales events are advertised through the classifieds and on a direct-mail basis— once you get your name on some lists, you get invited to other events.

You also can obtain referrals to auctioneers by asking local bank officers or attorneys who handle business liquidations or bankruptcy situations. Many commercial auctioneers maintain lists of individuals and companies seeking particular types of auctions and sales. They are generally willing to add you to their mailing list, but don't be surprised at the number of liquidation auctions held annually.

Auctions Offer Real Bargains. Consider the various ways one might arrive at a price for a desk:

- There is the price of purchasing such an item new from an office furniture supply firm.
- There is the price of buying a desk from another business that has time to advertise and sell it because it is moving to new quarters, with all new office furnishings.

- There is the liquidation price of a desk at an open bankruptcy auction that reflects the demand on that day in that place.

What could have been a $1,000 purchase one or two years ago is now a $200 liquidation bargain. Various types of inventory and commercial equipment sell for 25 to 50 cents on the dollar through used-equipment brokers and liquidation specialists.

While most people have limited experience negotiating prices, and then usually only for homes or automobiles, bankruptcy and liquidation auctions provide windows of insight into replacement values for a wide range of items, and the opportunity to bid on them. A note of caution: If you are new to auctions, be careful not to get caught up in the "group dynamics." Determine in advance what you want and scout comparable prices before attending. If you haven't attended an auction, consider training in becoming a prudent purchaser mandatory.

Chapter 3: Hot Tips and Insights

✓ The key to prudent purchasing is to become proactive in how you spend your money. How you make your purchases and control you inventory impacts your liquidity and may be your company's single largest cash trap.

✓ Develop multiple sources of supply.

✓ Continually seek purchasing intelligence. Are there associations in your field which sponsor group purchasing programs? How about merchant groups?

✓ Constantly seek favorable purchasing opportunities and then negotiate to make them even more favorable. Discipline yourself to be selective, wait, or say no, knowing that today's seemingly bargain price for goods may be exorbitant compared with tomorrow's. Become known as the buyer who hunts for values.

✓ If you run a small firm and are adept at purchasing, pass along this skill to your staff. Encourage the development of your staff's negotiating skills and enable them to gain experience.

✔ Effective purchasing and negotiating has less to do with price and quantity issues and more to do with human insight, personal interaction, and listening skills. Your suppliers need to make sales.

✔ Ask your suppliers, "What is your slowest sales month, and what kind of terms will you offer if I place a large order on the first of that month?"

✔ Don't jump whenever you're offered a discount for quantity purchases. Keep your purchase in perspective. A quantity discount for items you don't need to be holding is no bargain.

✔ When confronted with a quantity discount, ask yourself two questions: *Do I really need this much?* and *When can I reasonably expect to use or sell this?*

✔ Few things hurt a business more than cash resources locked up in dead inventory worth perhaps only a fraction of its cost. The longer you handle and store the items, the greater your risk of loss, damage, and danger that the model or technology will change.

✔ If you have the opportunity to take a prompt payment discount, take it if you have the cash; forget it if you don't.

✔ If you are asked for partial payment with or in advance of an order, always seek a lower price.

✔ Set up a simple filing system so you can send out checks just before they're due, but always on time.

✔ When you are desperate and have few options, pay bills in order according to their penalties.

✔ Negotiate payment arrangement with suppliers who are willing to "give" a little if it means keeping a steady, bill-paying customer on the books or making a big sale.

✔ Don't become short-sighted as to what *sustains* a positive cash flow. Quickly collecting the money you've earned and slowly paying what you owe is an overly simplistic view. Paying slow makes sense at times; however, it will not increase revenue, profitability, loyalty, or friendship among your suppliers or creditors, and it never eradicates the root causes of why you have to delay payment in the first place.

✓ Allow yourself to be courted as a customer. The person you are dealing with may not have authority to go below a certain price level, but may be able to offer other concessions. Push for them.

✓ Items purchased for business are either to be used, consumed, transformed, or resold; they are not to take up residence on your shelves.

✓ If you have inventory worth keeping but not worth storing on expensive leased property, inexpensively store it in leased warehouse space.

✓ If equipment is not visible to customers and otherwise need not represent the latest model, buy it second-hand.

✓ Call equipment-leasing businesses listed in the yellow pages to discuss the benefits of leasing versus owning equipment.

✓ Check out the current crop of superstores such as The Price Club, Staples, Micro Center, and Comp U.S.A. for attractive prices on office supplies and EDP equipment.

✓ Attend bankruptcy auctions, which offer you the opportunity to do some prudent purchasing of items usable in your business.

REDUCING UTILITY, PHONE, AND POSTAGE COSTS

It takes a very unusual mind to undertake the analysis of the obvious.

Alfred North Whitehead

Among the nagging business expenses that seem to escalate each year, utility, phone, and mailing costs for many businesses are the most troublesome. Although the level of service may not necessarily improve, the rates for these overhead expenses keep increasing. Fortunately, quite a bit can be done to lower costs while maintaining, or even increasing, the quality of service.

UTILITY COSTS

The Energy Crisis Never Ended

Despite the perception that the "energy crisis" passed in the 1970s, smaller businesses spend too much on utility costs and have few options for change. As a group, small businesses pay markedly higher rates per kilowatt hour of electricity than major industrial users, or even residential users. Although this information is readily available from the U.S. Department of Energy, the small business community hasn't seemed to notice and keeps biting the bullet without a squawk.

Some argue that the reason small businesses pay more for electricity than the industrial sector is that it is more costly for the utility companies to provide service to the commercial sector. Not so. Studies commissioned by the Department of Commerce and by the Small Business Administration have demonstrated that the net profit earned by electric utilities from the commercial sector was greater than that earned from the industrial sector, which is comprised largely of high energy users, including major corporations.

Various policy and rate-making standards have been introduced over the years. Unfortunately, the typical small business entrepreneur is not in a position to take advantage of declining bloc rates, time-of-day rates, season and interruptable rates, or any other options suggested.

Small business entrepreneurs seeking to reduce large energy bills do not always have the leeway to adapt energy consumption patterns to cheaper, off-peak hours. Their customers, suppliers, and employees may not appreciate 1 A.M. to 5 A.M. hours of operation. Regrettably, technology for storing electric power for off-peak use is not practical for most businesses.

Until some startling breakthrough occurs, small businesses are going to continue to light and power equipment with electricity, and heat and cool their companies with natural gas, oil, or electricity. It is going to cost a lot to do it, so let's see what can be done.

If you can reduce your energy consumption by 10 percent, you can realize an annual savings of between $150 to $1500, or more, depending on your normal consumption level (see Table 4.1).

Start at the Top

One of the most effective measures for stemming the tide of energy dollars consumed is to instill the notion of conservation and recycling of corporate resources among everyone who so much as turns on a light switch. You can make conservation part of your firm's culture—the smaller the firm, the faster the change.

Dollar Savings of 10 Percent Reduction in Energy Consumption

Kwh/Day Consumed	Daily Cost at $.085/Kwh	Daily Savings 10% Consumption Decrease	Annual Savings
5	$4.25	$.425	$155
10	8.50	.850	310
15	12.75	1.250	456
20	17.00	1.700	620
25	21.25	2.123	777
30	25.50	2.550	930
35	29.75	2.975	1081
40	34.00	3.400	1240
45	38.25	3.825	1396
50	42.50	4.250	$1551

Table 4.1.

Offer bonuses and visible rewards for notable conservation efforts on the part of staff. Circulate copies of your firm's energy bills each month as a reminder of your interest and commitment to reducing costs in this area.

In a soft real-estate market, if you rent your property, approach your landlord about concessions related to energy costs. These could include utility cost-sharing, utility/energy-related equipment retrofits, and installation of new energy control systems and monitors. You don't need to wait for Middle East flare-ups. Simply use your leverage as a valuable tenant.

In many parts of the country, the local electric and gas utility bills have a two-tier price on them. If you pay your bill within 10 or 20 days, the price is lower than it would be if you paid at the due date. As mentioned in Chapter 3, if you are a prompt payer, and are at or within a day or two of the cut-off date, you may be able to call the utility company and have them extend the discount time. Most utilities now have customer service representatives who answer billing inquiries and can call up your account records for the previous year on a computer screen. If your account has been paid promptly for the previous 12 months, they may be authorized to grant you the extension for a payment postmarked that day.

Cooling It on Over-Cooling

Excessive air-conditioning has become widely accepted in business. We justify it on the basis of moderate cost and high personal comfort. An air-conditioning system appropriately used, however, best serves as a mechanical means to ensure a reasonable comfort level—not as a summer "refrigeration unit."

The three most immediate and positive actions for helping to conserve energy when cooling your office include:

- Raising cooling temperatures
- Reducing the air-conditioning system load
- Moderating outside air intake

Raising Cooling Temperature. The simplest and fastest way to reduce consumption and the cost of cooling is to raise your thermostat by several degrees. Summer cooling in the 68 to 72 degree range is both wasteful and unnecessary. With a proper air flow and ventilation system, you and your staff can be quite comfortable at 73 or 74 degrees, and in some cases, reasonably comfortable up to 77 degrees.

By raising the temperature level, your cooling unit operates less, and electrical consumption decreases. For each degree the temperature is raised, cooling costs are reduced by approximately four percent. A home-based business entrepreneur in North Carolina reduced her energy consumption by 4600 kilowatt hours, resulting in several hundred dollars of savings, by moving the thermostat from 71 to 75 between April 1 and October 31 when the outdoor temperature was often above 80 degrees. The comfort level inside her 2400-square-foot home was affected only slightly.

Reducing Your Air-Conditioning System Load. With a central air-conditioning system, you can reduce your consumption for cooling by 20 percent. Cooling is seldom needed when space is unoccupied, such as in vacant offices, storage rooms, basements, and so forth, so close the vents and doors in areas where cooling is not necessary. Also reduce energy consumption by switching from incandescent to fluorescent lighting [see table 4.3], which also helps to lower the ambient temperature of your office space.

Adding an economizer, a device that can be installed on air-conditioning systems, reduces the amount of electricity consumed for air-conditioning by using outside air for cooling when it is cool enough outside. Many rooftop air-conditioning units today, especially in newer buildings, are engineered to accept the economizers. The cost range is $2400 to $3200, including installation, but the investment pays back in less than three years through reduced electricity consumption and the resulting savings.

Consider installing an economizer if you operate in a region where air-conditioning is required at least six months of the year, or if you are open after dark when the air outside is cooler. Many building managers leave the air-conditioning on all night, over weekends, and during holidays. By installing a seven-day clock, one can guarantee turnoff times and ensure that the system cranks up 60 to 90 minutes prior to occupancy so that the space will be comfortable when building tenants arrive.

Unless you're dealing with a heat-pump system, the old argument about more energy being lost when the air-conditioning system is turned off and on, particularly in light of today's better insulated buildings, is unfounded.

An efficient cooling system switched on only 30 minutes before you arrive at work will result in an overall reduction in energy consumption and yield nearly the same comfort level as if it had been on all night. Table 4.2 shows cost savings resulting from a 20-percent reduction in air-conditioning use.

Moderate Outside Air Intake.   Excessive intake of outside air for ventilation increases the cost of air-conditioning and heating. Since the energy consumption associated with air-conditioning and heating outside air is high, you'll want to ensure that minimum outside air is introduced into your office. Depending on the type of ventilation equipment you have, the reduction may be made by shutting off a fan, re-adjusting damper positions, or

**Monthly Air-Conditioning Cost Reduction
with 20 Percent Decreased Use**

Normal Use, Kwh/Month	Savings at Various Costs per Kilowatt Hour			
	$.06	$.08	$.10	$.12
500 Kwh	$6	$8	$10	$12
1000 Kwh	12	16	20	24
1500 Kwh	18	24	30	36
2000 Kwh	24	32	40	48
2500 Kwh	30	40	50	60
3000 Kwh	36	48	60	72
3500 Kwh	42	56	70	84
4000 Kwh	48	64	80	96
4500 Kwh	54	72	90	108
5000 Kwh	$60	$80	$100	$120

Table 4.2.

rearranging pulleys to reduce fan speeds. Economizers can also be used in conjunction with these other steps to reduce the intake of outside air.

You can modify the control systems and dampers of most older rooftop cooling units so that they shift when it is more economical to use outside air, instead of employing the higher-energy-consuming compressor/refrigeration cycle.

If you are located in a newer or high-rise structure, you may question why the most energy-efficient equipment was not originally installed. Often, but not necessarily, it is because construction costs dictated the developer's equipment selection—not downstream energy-consumption levels and costs. Whether or not you own the building, equipment modification should be performed by heating and cooling contractors, after discussion with equipment suppliers (and your leasing management firm, if applicable). Most contractors and vendors can recommend the appropriate system for achieving reduced energy consumption for cooling, installation costs, and length of payback.

When you take control of the situation and inform contractors of your desire to reduce energy consumption, you will find that you can be accommodated, and in nearly every instance, your initial out-of-pocket costs are repaid usually in three years or less, with increased savings thereafter.

Beyond Central Heating and Cooling.   Of all the devices and appliances that consume electricity, your water heater uses the most. In one year, even if your firm is nonindustrial and not a restaurant, you still may use up to 3000 kilowatt hours. By comparison, a frost-free refrigerator uses 2250 kilowatt hours; a room air conditioner, 860 kilowatt hours; a gas or electric range and oven, 700 kilowatt hours.

The most economical and energy-conserving solution is to install an inexpensive timer, available in any hardware store, that turns the water heater off and on again at your discretion. Timers cost around $20.00 to $25.00. By automatically shutting off the water heater all night and resuming an hour before you open, you can reduce your energy consumption by 20 to 25 percent at a minimum, annually saving hundreds of dollars.

If your space is so arranged, use room fans instead of air conditioners when fans will do. Used for the same number of hours, the fan will consume one-tenth the energy of the room air conditioner. You could run two or even three fans and still consume only a fraction of the energy that the room air conditioner uses. While it may not look chic, room fans for noncustomer areas could represent a breath of fresh air for your cash flow.

There is another way in which you can save on your monthly energy bill. If your facilities have a southern exposure, between October and April keep your blinds, shades, screens, and awnings open when the sun is out. The rays will help keep your office space warm, while the glass will keep out the colder air.

Trimming Energy Consumption with Lighting Control

Although you may not realize it, lighting represents a key area for energy conservation. In the days of lower-priced energy it was common to light all areas at a high level. Depending on your company's geographic location, the specifics of your facility, and when it was built, lighting may be a significant energy expense. Many firms today are overlit by modern efficiency standards, and others are inefficiently lit. Improved interior lighting can reduce energy consumption in this area by 15 to 18 percent.

The areas in your company that may be overlit include offices with a southern exposure, storage areas, supply rooms, garages, and the lunchroom. Here are some suggestions if you suspect that certain areas are overlit.

If you have fluorescent lighting, devices are available that allow two-tube fixtures to operate at half the output (and energy consumption) or allow them to operate with only one tube lit. You can install a phantom tube that will allow the fixture to function, but that actually consumes no electricity.

Where natural light is adequate, removing tubes is the easiest way to reduce light levels and is worth considering. Tubes should be taken out of the fixture to avoid flickering, and the ballast (which helps to both direct the current flow and steady the light) should be disconnected to achieve full savings. Otherwise, the ballast, which consumes 10 to 20 percent of the total fixture's energy, will continue to use some energy even though the fluorescent tubes are no longer in place.

When possible, replace incandescent lighting with fluorescent lighting. A 60-watt incandescent lightbulb is brighter than a 40-watt bulb, for example, as measured in lightness or "lumens." Yet, a 40-watt fluorescent light is 3.6 times as bright as a 60-watt bulb, emits less radiant heat, and consumes 33 percent less energy.

As Table 4.3 indicates, $2.00 to $3.00 savings per lamp can be achieved by replacing existing lamps with energy-saving lamps. If you have a hundred or more lamps in your store or warehouse, the savings can add up quickly.

It is not true that fluorescent lights should not be switched off when not in use. Studies show that if such lighting is not needed for as little as 10 minutes, it pays to shut it off. With all lighting, put stickers on switches reminding employees to "shut off" or "turn off" when not in use. The savings will accrue.

Energy Savings from Relamping

Replace	With	And Save (Watts/Lamp)	Annual $ Savings per Lamp
4-foot fluorescent	4-foot energy-saving equivalent	6	1.32
8-foot fluorescent	8-foot energy-saving equivalent	12	2.64
8-foot high-output fluorescent	8-foot high-output energy-saving equivalent	15	3.31
40-watt incandescent	36-watt, equivalent light output	4	.88
75-watt incandescent	69-watt, equivalent light output	6	1.32
150-watt incandescent	143-watt, equivalent light output	7	1.55
150-watt floodlamp	75-watt elliptical reflector (ER) flood lamp	75	16.59

Note: Assume that lamps are in use 10 hours per day at 9.5 Kwh. Shut off all fixtures when not in use.

Table 4.3.

Footcandles Light the Way. With incandescent lighting, to reduce existing light levels by 50 percent, install bulbs of one-half the wattage, and where possible, lower overhead fixtures to achieve adequate task lighting. In areas where concentrated work is done, 75 to 160 "footcandles" of lighting energy is desirable, compared to hallways where as little as 30 footcandles is ample.

Here is the formula for calculating footcandles: There are about 40 footcandles in one watt per square foot. Two uncovered 100-watt bulbs at ceiling height in an office measuring 12 feet by 12 feet, yield 55.5 footcandles:

$$\frac{2 \times 100 \text{ watts} \times 40}{12 \times 12} = 55.5 \text{ footcandles}$$

However one 60-watt bulb suspended three feet above a work area measuring three feet by five feet, yields 160 footcandles:

$$\frac{1 \times 60 \text{ watts} \times 40}{3 \times 5} = 160 \text{ footcandles}$$

Consider Life-Cycle Costs. Although bulbs of different wattage may have fairly similar initial prices, their life-cycle costs can be substantially different. As a general principle, replace all old bulbs with low-energy bulbs—they are electrically and mechanically interchangeable with your present lamps and use up to 20 percent less electricity. Available from manufacturers and some retailers, their purchase price is more than offset by the overall savings, as shown in Table 4.4.

Don't confuse low-energy bulbs with the "long-life" bulbs that are on the market. Long-life bulbs actually use more energy than ordinary bulbs in generating the same amount of light. An electrical supplier can provide information on the various brands and specifications for both fluorescent and incandescent low-energy lighting.

Be sure to clean all your lights and fixtures monthly. Dust and

The Real Cost of Lighting

Type		Purchase $ +	Energy $ =	Life cycle cost (8.5/Kwh)
Standard bulb:	100 watts 750 hours	$0.75	$6.38	$7.13
Standard bulb:	75 watts 750 hours	$0.75	$4.79	$5.54
Low-energy bulb:	69 watts 750 hours	$1.00	$4.39	$5.39

Table 4.4.

dirt can block five to 10 percent of the usable light. When renovating or painting your office interior, use white or other light colors to improve light quality.

To ensure you are not overlooking any part of your lighting scheme, review your total lighting use. As with heating and cooling units, automatic timers are available to put you in control of your lighting.

Utility Bill Auditing

There is growing concern among many entrepreneurs that the charges on the utility bills they receive do not reflect actual use. A St. Louis-based firm named Auditel Marketing Systems is one of a number of companies that will audit both your energy and telephone-related bills, with the goal of saving you money. The company states that they have been able to achieve savings for *four out of five clients* that they accept. They put forth the following points:

- Utility customers seldom are able to choose the lowest tariff classification to which they are entitled (from among hundreds the utility maintains).
- Utility rates, particularly for volume users, are negotiable.
- Utility and phone overcharges can be collected, even years after the errors occurred.

If you presume that utility bills you receive may be suspect, the odds are with you. By all means, audit your bills.

Company Vehicles and Garage

If you or your delivery or sales staff drive 10,000 miles per year and average 20 miles per gallon of gasoline, you are consuming 500 gallons of gasoline, which adds these harmful by-products to the environment:

- 3 to 10 pounds of soot,
- 5 to 20 pounds of nitrogen and sulfuric acids,

- 50 ounces or more of insoluble lead salts, if your car uses leaded gasoline, and
- as much as 20 ounces of hydrochloric acid.

We don't suggest reducing the effectiveness of your delivery or sales effort. However, can you reduce corporate driving by 20 percent? Order supplies by telephone, fax and mail more frequently than you have in the past. Let the postal or delivery services transport goods to you.

What about ensuring that all vehicles are operating efficiently? The average American commutes 157,598 miles to work during the course of a career, the equivalent of traveling more than six times around the world, and that doesn't include miles traveled during the workday.

American Automobile Association surveys of vehicles spot-checked routinely reveal that one vehicle in four needs a tune-up, one car in three needs at least a quart of oil, one car in three has underinflated tires, and one car in two needs a new air filter. If your staff drives as part of operations, hereafter consider it your civic, if not environmental, responsibility to keep company vehicles in A-1 condition.

TELECOMMUNICATION COSTS

Keeping Phone Costs on Hold

Never before have businesses been faced with such a wide array of cost-saving communications. However, most businesses are basically unaware of the choices available to them, and with good reason. There are the good old standbys like WATS lines and 800 numbers, a wide proliferation of long-distance companies, special systems for fax transmissions and conference calls, and volume discount offerings, to name just a few options.

As a result of this lack of awareness (and more than a bit of bewilderment), more than 90 percent of businesses **overpay** for their telecommunications systems. The once relatively simple process of selecting and installing a phone system has become a major source of unnecessarily high expenses.

To get an idea of the wealth of services available, take a look at just one particular segment: the long-distance market. Several services are available to you. Among them are:

AT&T Pro WATS. Provides discounts of between 10 to 26 percent to businesses that spend between $50 and $2500 per month. Service costs $5 a month.

AT&T WATS. Requires a dedicated line. Provides discounts between 12 to 30 percent on direct-dialed calls to companies spending more than $300 a month.

AT&T 800 Ready Line. Requires no special line and has discounts available based on volume and time of call.

MCI Vision. Flat-rate pricing regardless of distance.

MCI 800 Service. Volume discounts on incoming calls.

MCI 900 Service. Caller-paid long-distance service.

U.S. Sprint Dial 1 WATS. Provides discounts to companies spending more than $100 a month and requires no special lines, with some volume discounts available.

U.S. SprintFAX. Allows transmission to several locations simultaneously.

The above information represents merely a small cross-section of available telecommunications options and is by no means a complete list. When you attempt to get details regarding pricing and availability in your region, the local representative of each company supplies you with more information and options. Often you end up more confused, or worse, sold on the wrong system for you.

Educate Yourself

In light of the plethora of choices available, it's no surprise that even top managers within the telecommunications industry emphasize education as the first step toward reducing telephone costs. First, figure out your long-distance "traffic patterns." What is the volume of your company's calls, the length of each call, distances, primary calling areas, the time(s) of most of your calls, and so on? Only then can you sort out your most cost-efficient options.

You can change options whenever you have reason to believe

a change would be cost-effective. The number of choices is so large that you can easily feel intimidated by the thought of a change. Keep monitoring your patterns and don't act as if you're locked into an option you selected earlier.

An obvious cost cutting activity is to review your telephone and telecommunications bills each month. Phone companies are not infallible, and mistakes do occur—more often than they care to admit. It's not difficult to transpose a digit that ends up costing you more than you should be billed for.

In taking a good, hard look at the equipment and services you are using and trying to determine whether or not they match your company's needs as well as possible, rather than attempt such an analysis in-house, consider engaging the services of a telecommunications consultant. It's up-front money that can pay for itself many times over in long-term savings.

Through such analysis you can ascertain whether certain options will save you money. For example, Pete Silver, a marketing consultant and writer/speaker, points out several areas you may be able to get greater services at less cost than you thought:

Voice/data switches. Unless you use your fax machine night and day, you can eliminate the expense of a dedicated phone line by getting a switch.

Distinctive ring patterns. Another way to eliminate a second line is to subscribe to a service that allows you to have as many as four numbers on one line. You can identify the phone number by its assigned "ring pattern."

Local phone number in distant cities. Suppose that a sizable number of your customers live in one specific area (out of your immediate calling area) and you want to maintain a strong "local" presence in that distant market. If you employ remote call forwarding, your customers can dial a local number that is then forwarded to your own business number.

800 numbers. Only slightly more costly than the remote is the well-known 800 service, which allows your customers to call your business at no charge to them. An 800 number may be preferable to a remote call forward service if your market is widespread and you don't feel it necessary to maintain an image of local presence.

As you conduct your analysis of your telecommunications system, you may find other features valuable to your business—and make the cost of the analysis well worth its fee. You can arrange for a one-time review (for a one-time fee) that identifies present causes of overpayment and recommends solutions and areas of opportunity for the immediate future. (See also the earlier section in this chapter, "Utility Bill Auditing.")

You can also work with a telecommunications consulting service on a regular basis. Then a consultant can offer an initial review and recommendations and undertake ongoing monitoring of calling patterns, rate changes, and new services. Either way, the savings can be significant, and given the growing importance and complexity of telecommunications options, many businesses are actively seeking telecommunications consultants. To aid in your search, call, write, or fax:

Society of Telecommunications Consultants
4248 Park Glen Road
Minneapolis, MN 55416
(612) 927-6144
(612) 929-1318 FAX

Telemanagement Systems, The High-Tech Approach

Another option for monitoring your phone use and determining the best system for your business is through microcomputer software. Companies are beginning to reap the benefits of high-tech monitoring systems. As a result of the findings from using its PC and telemonitoring software, for example, a Detroit-based company eliminated three of its seven WATS lines and blocked certain numbers out of its system, including "Dial-a-date," sports-information, three pay-for-use "900" numbers, and the phone number for an out-of-state race track. The owner of the business, who paid $4,500 for the program, expects to recoup his costs within three years.

A New York company, Newcastle Communications, distributes a system that can be attached directly to your telephone system for just $1,800. Another system in that same price range is available from Complementary Solutions, Inc., in Atlanta, and it runs on an IBM compatible. In addition to automatically collecting call data, the system also includes information on phone tariffs. To keep current, for an extra fee customers may also arrange to have periodic updates sent automatically.

Often, the mere presence of such monitoring systems will dissuade employees from making excessive and long-distance personal phone calls. You'll not only save money but increase staff productivity as well. You may be able to achieve a drop in personal phone calls of 15 to 30 percent or more.

Educate your employees about the cost and capabilities of your telecommunications system. Even today, a common belief among staff is that calls placed on a WATS line are somehow "free." Show your employees how the phone bills are computed and how their calls affect the bottom line. Insist that your employees direct-dial long-distance calls. Operator-assisted calls send phone bills through the roof.

A telecommunications system can be used to double-check phone bills. One company discovered $2,750 worth of unfounded charges and received a refund. That alone paid for the system. Once again, the wide range of choices in the telemanagement system can be overwhelming. One possibility is to hire a consultant on a one-time, one-fee basis to research and recommend a particular system for your company's use.

By all measures, the key to a cost-efficient phone system, then, is knowledge. Familiarize yourself with various payment plans and calling features, monitor your company's phone patterns, and match the equipment you buy to the services you need.

POSTAGE COSTS

Licking Postage Costs

The cost of first-class postage has gone up, but your overall mailings need not. In this section we'll explore ways to get your mail and packages delivered on time without draining your cash.

You're probably fairly knowledgeable when it comes to options available through private, commercial express mail services. Nearly everyone in the working world knows how to

"FEDEX" a package for next-day delivery. However, *overuse* of express mail has had diminishing impact on recipients. Use it when you *have to*, but realize that it makes more sense in many instances, and generates comparable "receiver impact," to use the U.S. Postal System—for all its troubles—if you know how to use the system effectively.

Wading Through Standard Mailing Options

Here is a brief, alphabetical description from the U.S. Postal Service of a wide variety of standard services to safeguard, protect, and document your packages. This roster may convince you that using Uncle Sam's mail service can be cost-effective after all.

Express Mail Service.   This is the Post Office's fastest service, and is fairly comparable to commercial services. "Express Mail Next Day Service" provides several options for both private and business customers who require overnight delivery of letters and packages. To use Express Mail Next Day Service, take your shipment to any designated Express Mail post office, generally by 5 P.M., or deposit it in an Express Mail collection box. Your mail will be delivered to the addressee by 3 P.M. the next day (weekends and holidays included). In many cities, Express Mail deliveries are made before noon.

There are over 26,000 post offices and 10,000 special Express Mail collection boxes in which you can deposit your pieces. Also, your letter carrier can accept prepaid Express Mail shipments at the time your mail is delivered. The Post Office will supply you with mailing containers (envelopes, boxes, and tubes) and the necessary mailing labels free of charge. If you're mailing say, a 30 page report, Express Mail costs several dollars less than nearly all commercial express services.

First-Class Mail.   Such mail is designed for letters, post cards, postal cards, greeting cards, and personal notes, and for sending checks and money orders. You can't insure ordinary First-Class Mail. However, additional services such as certificates of mailing, certified return receipts, and restricted delivery can be purchased at the option of the mailer.

If your First-Class Mail is not letter size, make sure it is marked "First Class" or use a green-bordered large envelope.

Forwarding Mail.   When you move, fill out a "Change of Address" card in advance at your local post office. When possible, notify your post office at least one month before your move. First-Class Mail is forwarded for free. Magazines, newspapers, and other second-class mail are forwarded at no charge for 60 days from the effective date of a change-of-address order. Your post office has information about holding mail, temporary changes of address, and forwarding and return of other classes of mail.

Mailgram® Service.   "Mailgram" is a registered trademark of Western Union Corporation. Mailgram® service is an electronic message service offered by Western Union that provides next-day Postal Service delivery for messages sent to any address in the United States. The messages are transmitted for delivery with the next business day's mail. You can send Mailgram® messages by calling Western Union and dictating your message to the operator, or you can use your office Telex or TWX.

Priority Mail.   This is First-Class Mail weighing more than 12 ounces and up to 70 pounds, with size limitations. The Post Office provides free "Priority Mail" stickers. Insurance (discussed below) can be purchased on Priority Mail.

Third-Class Mail.   Also referred to as bulk business or advertising mail, Third-Class Mail may be sent by anyone, but is used most often by large mailers. This class includes printed material and merchandise weighing less than 16 ounces. There are two rate structures for this class: single piece and bulk rate. Also, individuals may use this class for mailing lightweight parcels and insurance can be purchased, at the option of the mailer, to cover loss or damage of articles mailed at the Third-Class rate.

Protecting and Documenting Your Mail

Certified Mail.   This provides a mailing receipt, and a record of delivery is maintained at the recipient's post office. You can also pay an additional fee for a return receipt to indicate proof of delivery. For valuables and irreplaceable items, the Postal Service recommends using insured or registered mail.

Collect on Delivery (COD).   COD is useful when you want to collect for merchandise (up to a maximum of $500) when it is delivered. COD service may be used for merchandise sent by First-Class, Third-Class, or Fourth-Class Mail. The merchandise must have been ordered by the addressee. The Postal Service includes insurance protection against loss or damage within their fee. COD items also may be sent as registered mail.

Insurance.   Insurance can be purchased on registered mail up to a maximum of $25,000 and up to $500 for Third- and Fourth-Class Mail and for merchandise mailed at the Priority Mail or First-Class Mail rates. With articles insured for more than $25, a receipt-of-delivery card is signed by the recipient and filed at the delivery post office. The amount of insurance coverage for loss is the actual value, less depreciation, and no payments are made for sentimental losses or for any expenses incurred as a result of the loss.

Registered Mail.   The Postal Service regards this as their most secure mailing option. It is designed to provide added protection for valuable and important mail. Postal insurance may be purchased at the option of the mailer, up to a maximum of $25,000 in coverage, and return receipt and restricted delivery services are available for an additional fee. Registered articles are controlled from the point of mailing to delivery. First-Class postage is required on registered mail.

Restricted Delivery.   Except for Express Mail service, you can request restricted delivery when purchasing return receipt service. Restricted delivery means that delivery is made only to the addressee or to someone who is authorized in writing to receive mail for the addressee. Restricted delivery mail addressed to officials of government agencies, members of the legislative and judicial branches of federal and state governments, members of the diplomatic corps, minors and individuals under guardianship can be delivered to an agent without written authorization from the addressee.

Return Receipt. This is the your proof of delivery and is available for mail that you send by COD or Express Mail, is insured for more than $25, or which you register or certify. The return receipt shows who signed for the item and the date it was delivered. For an additional fee, you can get an exact address of delivery or request restricted-delivery service.

Special Delivery. You can buy Special Delivery service for all classes of mail except bulk Third-Class. It provides for delivery, even on Sundays and holidays, during hours which extend beyond the hours for delivery of ordinary mail. This service is available to all customers served by city carriers and to other customers within a one-mile radius of the delivery post office. Note that Special Delivery may be delivered by your regular carrier if it is available before he or she departs for morning deliveries. You have to call your post office to find out about the availability of Special Delivery service in the area to which you are mailing.

International Mail. You can send air and surface mail to virtually all foreign countries. There are four types of international mail:

1. Letters and Cards—includes letters, letter packages, light-weight aerogrammes, and post cards.
2. Other Articles—includes printed matter, matter for the blind, and small packets.
3. Parcel Post.
4. Express Mail International Service.

Registry service with limited reimbursement protection is available for letters, cards, and other articles to many nations, and insurance is available for parcel post to most countries.

Reducing Paper Costs

Before leaving this chapter, let's briefly cover an additional area of overhead expense. In the United States, each adult generates 3.5 lbs. of waste and refuse per day, or one ton per person per year. Here, the need for conservation techniques and effective recycling on the household level is at epidemic proportions, although scarcely one percent of solid waste makes its way through the recycling process. The nation's landfills, inland waterways, and coastal areas are spewing forth the inevitable results of decades of abuse.

To reduce paper costs and support the environment, reuse all 8.5″ by 11″ sheets and larger business envelopes when possible. If an envelope sent to you arrives in reasonable shape, put a gummed label over the original label, place your stamps or postage meter sticker over the originals and remail the envelope. To legitimize envelope recycling, order a rubber stamp from a local printer that reads:

"RECYCLING ENVELOPES
SAVES TREES"

and stamp it in the lower left-hand corner. If even 10 percent of envelopes are recycled, your savings add up.

Reuse all pieces of paper that still have one good side. A company in Lexington, Kentucky keeps a bin by its large, high-speed copier so that when employees err or overcopy, the "ruined" sheets are collected, cut, and reused as scratch pads. Another company requests that its employees simply draw a long diagonal slash on the unusable side of the copier paper that signals to others that the blank side of the sheet is meant to be reused.

You don't have to let overhead expenses nibble away at your cash. You can keep the cash traps in check through innovation and simply by remaining alert to lower cost options.

Chapter 4: Hot Tips and Insights

✔ Instill the notion of conservation and recycling of corporate resources among all your employees. You can make conservation part of your firm's culture—the smaller the firm, the faster the change.

✓ Offer bonuses and visible rewards for notable conservation. Circulate copies of your firm's energy bills each month to remind the employees of your interest and commitment to reducing costs in this area.

✓ Approach your landlord about concessions related to energy costs, including utility cost-sharing, utility/energy-related equipment retrofits, and installation of new energy control systems and monitors.

✓ The three most immediate and positive actions for helping to conserve energy when cooling your office include raising cooling temperatures, reducing your air-conditioning system load, and moderating outside air intake.

✓ Install an economizer if you operate in a region where air-conditioning is required at least six months of the year, or if you are open after dark when the air outside is cooler.

✓ When you inform contractors of your desire to reduce energy consumption, you will find that in nearly every instance, your initial out-of-pocket costs can be recaptured, usually in three years or less, with increased savings thereafter.

✓ Your company may be overlit in offices with a southern exposure, storage areas, supply rooms, garages, and the lunchroom.

✓ Reduce corporate driving by 20 percent by ordering supplies by telephone, fax, or mail more frequently than you have in the past. Let the postal or delivery services transport goods to you.

✓ Ensure that all vehicles are operating efficiently. American Automobile Association surveys of vehicles spot-checked routinely reveal that one vehicle in four needs a tune-up, one car in three needs at least a quart of oil, one car in two needs a new air filter.

✓ Education is the first step toward reducing telephone costs. Figure out your long-distance "traffic patterns"—the volume of your company's calls, the length of each call, distances, primary calling areas, and the time(s) of most of your calls.

✓ Engage the services of a telecommunications consultant to achieve your most effective system. It's an investment that can pay for itself many times over in long-term savings.

✓ Use microcomputer software to reap the benefits of high-tech telephone monitoring systems. Often, the presence of such monitoring systems will dissuade employees from making excessive and long-distance personal phone calls.

✓ Educate your employees about the cost and capabilities of your phone system. Even today, a common belief among staff is that calls placed on a WATS line are somehow "free."

✓ Overuse of express mail has had diminishing impact on recipients. Use it when you *have to*, but realize it makes more sense in many instances to use the Post Office.

✓ Get thoroughly acquainted with the numerous, sometimes poorly promoted and explained services of the U.S. Postal System.

✓ To reduce paper costs and support the environment, reuse all 8.5" by 11" sheets and large envelopes when possible.

5

GETTING THE MOST
FROM YOUR BANK

Let me smile with the wise, and feed with the rich.

Samuel Johnson

In the course of your business, it may be fitting and proper to seek debt-financing, particularly if you're in a growth stage. Most banks want to make loans, but they have a whole series of rituals they go through and want you to go through, before they'll cut the check. Generally, the longer the payback period for a loan, the higher the risk to the bank. To protect itself, the bank is naturally interested in the profits that you will generate. Banks are also keenly interested in knowing if you have a guarantee from the Small Business Administration, since that greatly reduces their risk.

You must offer personal guarantees and, considering the length and complexity of some of the loan documents these days, in more ways than you will ever know. The bank will take your personal assets, if it has to. If your note has been cosigned by another, his or her assets will also be under lien.

If your loan is specifically for the purchase of assets, the bank will take the first position; that is, they get the assets should you default. However, they also will take the second position on accounts receivables, inventory, or other assets. This is called an assignment and, in the case of accounts receivables, would be called "a blanket position on receivables."

A cash trap that ensnares far too many entrepreneurs is seeking funds after they *have* to have them. To get over the reflexive tendency to ask for money too late in the game, consider that it takes at least three times longer to get a loan than most loan applicants contemplate when first identifying the need to get a loan.

An important part of any loan application is the financial statement. This is where you convince the banker that you are worth the risk. Include the assets you can provide as collateral. In establishing the value of your assets, don't inflate them, but be sure to give yourself the benefit of any doubt. Many banks are likely to downgrade the value of your collateral by as much as a third to limit their exposure.

HITTING A MOVING TARGET

Whether in a start-up situation or further downstream, obtaining a loan requires the same kinds of skills needed to hit a moving target. The inherent lags in loan application procedures and reviews, combined with other uncertainties as to actual start-up date, distribution of funds, and the like, means that even with a successful application, you will likely get the loan at a time not well synchronized with your plans.

Start preparing your loan package the nanosecond you perceive a forthcoming need. For start-ups, which face a tough road for getting a loan at all, six months' to a year's advance preparation is not uncommon. Your ability to offer a detailed, credible business plan is of prime importance when seeking a loan. Specifically, when seeking debt, you will have to pinpoint the following:

- how much money you need
- over what period
- what security or collateral will be provided
- how the funds will be used
- when and how you will pay the money back

Not surprisingly, the most effective way to answer these questions and to provide a graphic overview of your situation is to produce both a short- and long-term cash-flow analysis.

An axiom in seeking a loan is that whatever amount you are seeking is probably too little. The inherent danger of asking for too much is that you may be rejected because the financial institution doesn't see a way to cover itself for the full amount of the loan. The danger in asking for too little is twofold: (1) you may actually receive that amount and find it inadequate, and thus be in an awful cash trap because you blew your big chance for adequate financing; and (2) bankers are more likely to reject applicants that ask for too little because these applicants appear to have an unrealistic view of the situation.

Between asking for too much or too little, you are better off asking for too much. The banker may knock down the amount you seek and offer you a lesser figure. If you ask for too little based on your actual need, and this is apparent to those reviewing your loan package, you have no retreat. When you hear the words "based on your situation this amount will not be adequate," you have already indicated your inability to identify your own financial needs. The only question the loan officer will have at this point is (unvoiced), "What are your other managerial shortcomings?"

FAMILIARIZE YOURSELF WITH OTHER SOURCES

For peace of mind and negotiating leverage, it makes sense to familiarize yourself with other available financing sources before walking into the bank. On a personal basis, there are your own savings, life-insurance loan programs, friends, relatives, and yes, taking out a second mortgage on your home.

If you've been in business for a while, asset-based financial measures include loans secured by accounts receivables, inventories, or fixed assets; leasing of fixed assets; or transfer of accounts receivables to another party.

Debt capital also can be raised through finance companies, SBA guaranteed loans both with or without a commercial bank's participation, federal loans for businesses in high employment or undeveloped areas, loans from other businesses such as insurance companies, or industrial revenue bonds.

Lines of Credit.   Instead of seeking a loan each time you need cash, you could seek a line of credit. If you have developed a sound banking relationship, obtaining a line of credit need not be difficult. As with any loan, the best time to seek this form of financing is when you don't really need it. Much of the same criteria used in judging your conventional loan application will be used in judging the line-of-credit application.

Venture Capital.   Raising capital, either debt or equity, is tough. Most venture capitalists prefer to invest in companies in leading-edge industries. Venture capitalists have been known to invest in companies in the blueprint stage, when products or services are being conceptualized, when second-round financing is being sought, or when the company is undergoing expansion, experiencing a turnaround, or undertaking a buyout.

The best way to favorably influence a venture capitalist is to offer a product or service with a competitive edge in a rapidly growing industry and to assemble a solid management team with each member very experienced in his field. Your ability to demonstrate commitment to the success of your firm, put in long hours, and use your own capital are key elements of your venture capital proposal. Be sure to indicate previous mistakes, along with lessons that you have learned. You're certainly not perfect, and your investors want a balanced picture.

While a small number of venture capitalists specialize in making investments in the $55,000 to $350,000 range, generally investments of under $500,000 or $1,000,000 are *not* attractive to most venture capitalists. Industries such as medical electronics, laser optics, data processing, telecommunications, waste treatment, and energy conservation seem to be of great interest to venture capitalists. The biggest potential returns are seen through investing in firms with a leading-edge product in a growth industry.

CULTIVATING RELATIONS WITH LOAN OFFICERS

Money magazine conducted a random survey of bankers around the country a few years back, and each responded that the most important financial move a customer can make is to establish a working relationship with a banker. Many business owners have discovered that a strong relationship with a banker can be crucial for avoiding cash crunches.

In smaller and medium-sized banks set a goal of introducing yourself to the vice president for business development, one or two of the commercial loan officers, and the local branch manager. In a larger bank make it a point to know the regional commercial loan officers as well as the branch manager and business development officers. In this era of aggressive bank marketing, as a potential loan recipient, creator of jobs, payer of taxes, and pillar of the community it makes good sense to know these officers well before you ever ask for a loan.

One successful executive from Oakland comments, "I have always taken my banking business to the nearby branch of a major bank in my community. I target the branch manager—he's less likely to turn over than others. I develop a special banking relationship with him. I actually send my deposits addressed to him, although I fully realize that he immediately hands these over to a teller.

"The bank can't be a foreign institution to me, and I don't want to be just another customer to them. I work at maintaining this relationship, yet I rarely visit the bank myself, preferring to use the phone, mail, and staff members to handle my transactions.

"I am constantly sharing my business plans with the branch manager and, when I need help, I call on him. If a competitor's interest rates go down one-quarter percent, I don't get excited or skip to the next bank, because I've come to learn that over the long haul, a few percentage points in either direction are not nearly as important as the relationship I am building. To be sure, the branch manager knows my views on this."

Don't wait until the handwriting is on the wall (*and ceiling and floor*). It's bad form to introduce yourself to a loan officer, begin to talk about your business, and then say, "Everything is going well, can you lend me X-amount?" and "I need it as soon as possible." This is not likely to win you any points. No one wants to go to bed with you on the first date. You certainly don't project the image of an effective planner.

Loan officers are eager to develop long-term client relationships and to provide additional services such as payroll management, financial systems, or pension management. The more he is able to get to know you, the more his perceived risk diminishes. Keep building the relationship so that the banker maintains an interest in you and your accounts and is responsive to your needs. If the bank is not responsive, go elsewhere.

AN UPWARD TREK—SECOND-ROUND FINANCING

Obtaining a loan for the second time from a bank can be much more difficult than the first time. Although you split a gut to get your first loan, those were the good old days. The irony of financing is that as revenues are increasing and the business is about to expand, it becomes most difficult to portray the business in a favorable light. As you well know, with increased revenues, expenditures for inventory, labor, and other variable costs such as commissions, delivery, and shipping all increase.

Since these expenditures are made prior to the actual revenue generation, financial statements of the business are likely to reflect a weakened position. Cash-flow projections may indicate an improved cash position several months in the future, with large cash deficits leading up to those months. Too many businesses fall into a giant cash trap and fail because of the lack of second-round financing.

TWO RELATIONSHIP CASES

Case 1.   Here's a look at a successful, growing banking relationship between the president of a dry-cleaning company and his local banker. He started with personal accounts and with help in financing the company's operations. The loans were used to secure equipment that offered returns over several years. He also patronized the bank for other services—checking, personal loans, a discount brokerage stock portfolio, and credit cards.

Later, the bank extended him a $75,000 line of credit, which he then took to support a $150,000 loan from a larger bank. That loan enabled him to buy out silent partners. After he took control of the company, its annual revenues increased by 23 percent, topping $456,000 thousand after three years. Several of the bank's staff were present at the dedication of a remodeled store.

After you've found a banker with whom you can build a relationship, you can't be complacent. When you have an effective relationship and are obtaining the loan you seek, keep the relationship vibrant by occasionally:

- paying loans off early
- becoming a shareholder in the bank
- sending them a new customer or two

Let's look at another case.

Case 2.   Harold M. was the head of a four-year-old advertising and public-relations firm in Miami. He started the business entirely on his own funds. After one year he sought a $22,000 loan to buy more equipment and offer a greater level of service. Harold got the loan at the same bank where he had maintained a personal savings account and a business checking account.

Beginning year three, Harold had three times as many employees as a year before and three times the payroll. He was doing a booming business and the size of his accounts receivables was steadily increasing. Harold had been in pursuit of two major clients, one for more than a year. Then, in the same week he landed both of them!

With such fortune also came new challenges. Harold would have to increase his staff by 50 percent. He also would have to acquire several pieces of equipment to handle the increase in business. Given all that was occurring, Harold made the decision to move into larger quarters. The new quarters carried a monthly rent 35 percent higher than he was presently paying.

Always an excellent planner and having maintained excellent relationships with his bank over the years, Harold took his loan officer to lunch one afternoon. Armed with the necessary financial projections and supporting information the loan officer needed to see, Harold requested a loan of $75,000 and a doubling of his line of credit.

They both left the lunch table that afternoon in good spirits and in full understanding and agreement with one another's positions. Harold knew that the loan was not a sure thing until it was *actually* approved, yet, to proceed with his plans, he had to make some basic assumptions. Over the next two weeks, Harold charted the coming six months for his firm.

One afternoon when he was busy working on something else, the loan officer called to tell him that the committee had decided against granting the loan. The words had only partially sunk in. Harold asked "What?" The loan officer commiserated. She was as surprised as Harold that the request was rejected. Harold pressed to find why he had been rejected but couldn't get a sufficient explanation.

Having time to reflect on what had occurred, Harold was stunned and embittered. For years he had been a faithful bank patron, had honored all loan commitments, and had kept his banker abreast of his progress on a regular basis. He was no stranger to the bank. His business was a success, and everyone involved with it knew it.

By any measure he could determine, his loan request was reasonable. What real risk did the bank have honoring his loan request? He could see none.

All this mental chatter was getting him nowhere; his bank had left him out in the cold. Harold was beset with the problem of having to find a new bank, establish a new relationship, and most importantly, procure the desired funds. He accepted this setback because he had no other choice.

In discussions with fellow business owners, he learned that many had experienced the same type of letdown. Exchanging information with others on which banks to contact, Harold was finally able to find a bank AND a loan officer who were willing to work with his business. Ultimately, Harold got the loan, 14 weeks after his initial quest.

His expansion plan temporarily thwarted, Harold muddled through much as he had done in the past. The long-term effects on his business will be negligible, but the short-term struggle was horrendous.

What of Fairness?   Fairness would dictate that the bank owes an extra measure of consideration to long-standing clients, and at least an explanation of loan rejections. This is simply not the case. Bank priorities change, bank personnel change, and the amount of funds available for making loans fluctuates. At any point along the trail, your application might be rejected based on circumstances that have less to do with the size and nature of your request than with the prevailing environment.

Always select your bank carefully. Examine them just as closely as they examine you. Find out who is on the board, who their officers are, the size of their assets, and the reputation they have in the community. What do they charge compared to other banks; what types of programs are available; and what is their relationship to others in your line of business?

Maintain a network of communications with peers and join those civic and community associations in which representatives from several banks are members. Never take your present bank for granted; they may let you down at any moment. This is not being defensive, just realistic. Ideally, you want to find a bank that will not only meet your needs now, but can stay with you and meet them later.

NEGOTIATING YOUR LOAN

If you've played your cards right, you can actually get favored treatment at your bank. By cultivating a relationship in advance, you can request and possibly get lower interest rates than the going rate on loans, and have other service costs eliminated. The better the loan officer understands your business—the more information he has on you in his file—the more effectively you'll be represented to the bank loan committee.

When it comes to actually negotiating the loan, start by whittling away at the extra fees. "Nonrefundable application fees, filing charges, and credit-check expenses should be covered under the bank's overhead, which is paid by interest," says ex-banker Edward Mrkvicka. You may also be able to reduce the interest rate by pledging stable collateral, such as stock or a certificate of deposit.

If you've done your homework and are aware of both alternative financing sources and, specifically, what other banks are charging, it's to your advantage and can be of help in bringing down your interest rate. "There are few threats as effective as taking your business elsewhere," says Mrkvicka, "especially if you have a name and rate from elsewhere that you can quote from that elsewhere."

If possible, try to avoid "loan" insurance, which is really term life insurance written as credit life insurance, on the principle of the borrower who has usually provided a personal guarantee of the loan which can cost you up to 10 percent of the principal and only serves to ensure that the lender gets paid if you die or become disabled. In most cases, banks get a 40 percent commission from insurance carriers on policies that they sell in connection with loans. "If the bank is adamant about being insured, you probably can do better by just taking out a term life-insurance policy from your own agent," says Mrkvicka.

In addition, see if you can arrange another party's collateral to receive a larger loan or more favorable rates. For example, perhaps a relative will serve as a cosigner. Above all, be prepared to argue every line item in the application to cut your cost or improve your chances, if need be. You have nothing to lose.

STRENGTHENING YOUR CREDIT RATING

Your credit rating is a valuable asset when you are applying for a loan or dealing with creditors, so work to maintain a solid rating. "It pays over and over again," says one entrepreneur who has not had a difficult time procuring loans. "When you have a solid credit rating, things work in your favor. People you have not met before are ready to offer loans or do business with you.

"In our company, if an outside party wants to check our credit rating or examine our P&Ls, we give it to 'em on a silver platter. More than once we have received loan terms that the banks earmark only for their best and longest-standing customers. We actually have gotten better terms than what we were originally shooting for."

So, how is your credit rating determined? At your request, your business's credit history and financial strength are determined by a credit reporter employed by a credit rating service. The rating is based on the amount and quality of information gathered by interviewing you and by consulting public records, banks and suppliers, and other sources.

You are requested to complete an extensive form so that accurate information about your company goes on file. Although it is time-consuming and tedious to answer dozens of questions, it is to your advantage to cooperate fully with the rating service.

What Credit Granting Organizations Look For

A company that undertakes a thorough credit rating, before extending credit to you examines the following areas:

- ☐ The character of principals, their reputation, and management ability. Are they conservative or venturesome? Do they seem intelligent? Do they have high living standards?

- ☐ Is the credit requested unreasonable or unusual for this type of business?

- ☐ What is the business location like, and what is the condition of the neighborhood?

- ☐ Is the credit information readily furnished, and are answers to the point and unevasive?

- ☐ Do the principals have other enterprises? Do these ventures enhance the credit risk?

- ☐ How does the highest credit line extended to a customer compare with the present request, under current business conditions?

- ☐ Is business insurance adequate? Has a safety check been made to reduce the hazards of fire and other disasters?

Suppliers' Credit Checks

Many suppliers undertake their own credit evaluation. In evaluating the credit of your firm, suppliers may:

- ☐ look for and analyze distress signals, such as partial payment being made, or notes offered in payment;
- ☐ check in advance for guarantees or securities available, should the circumstances suggest their need;
- ☐ examine your business hazards, personnel, sponsors, and links to other enterprises;
- ☐ check outside mortgages, liens, or control on the management by other creditors or interested parties;
- ☐ check to see if your operation is subject to unusual price-cutting and excessive risks, and if you are tied in with any other companies likely to affect risk;
- ☐ obtain the facts of any bankruptcies or receiverships mentioned in your credit application;
- ☐ check whether or not others have ever had to institute legal action for collection;
- ☐ search public records for judgments and other liens that may not have been mentioned in the customary sources of credit information;
- ☐ determine if there is any contest by insurance companies or underwriters about fire losses.

In addition, cash, accounts receivable, and inventory are investigated in detail by those checking your credit. Specific information sought includes the following.

Cash

- ☐ Is your money on deposit with a bank that also carries your outstanding loans? In such a case, the money is usually encumbered directly to the extent of that loan.
- ☐ How much of the available cash is earmarked for immediate payment of wages, dividends, bonuses, loans coming due, and purchase commitments for expansion programs?

☐ If there are unusually large cash balances, are there indications of inefficient use of capital?

☐ If there are unusually low cash balances, will assets, such as accounts receivable or inventories, have to be pledged for losses to the disadvantage of general creditors?

Accounts Receivable

☐ What portion of the receivables may be classed as "good," which can be counted on for payment when due, and what portion is "bad"?

☐ Which accounts are past due and why?

☐ What is the credit standing of each substantial past-due account or unusually large current account? Do sales and past-due accounts information match?

☐ Have some accounts been sold or assigned, without being so indicated?

Inventory

☐ Are inventories kept under control by means of accurate and detailed records?

☐ In consideration of seasonal changes or other factors, is the estimated liquidity of inventory sufficient?

The best approach is to deal honestly with credit rating services (as well as with suppliers who can extend credit, too). Avoid claims that cannot be substantiated and commitments that cannot be met. Show some financial weakness and maintain honesty rather than exhibit financial strength, only to be discovered later.

NEVER APPEAR DESPERATE

How do you obtain badly needed funds without appearing to have a great need for them? You do it by making your request for financial assistance as part of an overall business planning process, and not because you have to have it or else. You'll have to tread a fine line here. Bankers actively look for clues to see if you're in trouble.

Stability in your location and firm, as well as educational attainment, are to your advantage in asking for a loan. The strongest argument for lending money for a project, however, is a good project. Get others, such as your lawyer or accountant, to recommend you. You can also include various agreements with partners and pre-order agreements and other documents indicating that the project is actually going to begin and succeed. The underlying message that you want to present is that you are serious and know what you are doing, not that you are desperate and floundering.

If you have too much invested in fixed assets without corresponding revenues to justify them, or if you are overextended—constantly operating on a shoe string—all the alarms go off. Loans to officers or owners for nonbusiness purposes get you a quick rejection. Similarly, if you have a pile of unpaid bills, excessive officer salaries, or heavy inventories compared to sales, the loan officer and other creditors will be wary.

Of course, the strongest negative marks are bankruptcies, judgments, collections, patterns of late payments, delinquencies, or court claims, because these indicate that you might be a bad risk. Also, make sure you have no outstanding balance on student loans, even from 20 years ago. The loan committee is adamant about not granting loans to those who have defaulted on student loans.

Find out which credit bureaus your bank is using to get reports on you, and request your own copies. Then, if the report includes something you dispute, you can challenge it.

THE NEW BANKING RELATIONSHIPS

New banking relationships and arrangements are rapidly coming on line as banks scramble to keep pace with competitors, amidst new regulations in a rapidly changing society. Because your personal banking relationships carry over into the life of your business, let's examine what is available.

The ultimate in banking services for individuals is what is called private banking—basically a direct one-to-one, preferred relationship between the banker and you. Some banks offer qualifying clients, those with annual high incomes, speedy turnaround on loan applications, lower rates on larger lines of credit, and personalized investment advice. These banks will restructure your estate, review your will, and inventory your personal assets and liabilities. They can take this information to create a strategy to meet both your short- and long-term financial goals.

Private banking services and private banking-type services, however, are no longer only within the domain of the very rich and powerful. Increasingly, a wider range of customers are enjoying services such as:

- personalized estate planning,
- personalized stock brokerage,
- expedited loan processing, and
- 24-hour message reception.

As competition for banking business heats up, desirable, potentially long-term customers—described by some as "homeowners with children"—even in the $45,000 to $60,000 annual income range, can partake of a variety of private banking-type services. Often the key to gaining valuable additional services is simply to know enough to inquire about them.

One bank, headquartered in Richmond, Virginia, will assist customers with estate planning and accounts, perform custodial services, such as tracking the time-consuming details of customer investments, and provide regular reports and tax summaries. They'll also set up living and testamentary trusts and handle a variety of life-insurance programs, line-of-credit programs, and retirement plans.

For these customers, this bank will serve as register and transfer agent or exchange agent for corporate security transactions, and will serve as trust depository, including buying, selling, receiving, and delivering securities. The bank will even provide collection services.

Private banking services initially are established face-to-face.

Thereafter, mail, phone, facsimile, E-mail, and wire serve the customer well and almost exclusively. Account managers keep customers informed of new products, services, and rate variations. Some actively relay data they know or believe the customer is interested in receiving.

In any metropolitan area of at least 200,000 people, you can easily comparison-shop among a variety of banking institutions without leaving home. You can obtain the information you need over the phone by requesting and obtaining brochures.

In a matter of minutes you'll know if you've reached an unresponsive, noncustomer-oriented institution:

- They are hard to reach by phone.
- They are not readily able to discuss their services.
- There is no enthusiasm for your call.
- You feel as if you intruded on them by calling!

Customer-oriented banks that have developed comprehensive, private-banking-like services for middle-income earners are only too happy to let inquirers know about them. Conversely, you can tell in a matter of minutes when you're dealing with an unresponsive, nonconsumer-oriented bank if you can't reach them easily by phone. If your call is met with lukewarm interest or if the bankers aren't available to discuss their offerings, you should probably find somewhere else where you can do better.

If you presently lack the financial clout to rank the special treatment of true personal banking, you can still partake of "relationship banking." With the tightening banking market, many smaller banks are looking for the big customers of the future, and are banking on loyalty early on to carry over to a lucrative future.

This sort of reciprocity has worked for many business owners when they were starting out. Almost without exception, the whiz kids of the microcomputer industry cultivated bankers to finance their explosive growth.

Bankers also are making it easier to establish a strong banking relationship with them through bundled or packaged banking. With banking packages, you can combine their everyday checking accounts, loans, other lines of credit, and certificates of deposit. As customers decry fees imposed on most individual accounts—per-check fees, transaction fees, fees for obtaining quarterly statements—bundles have become increasingly popular with banks. Most banks require a few thousand in total deposits, a relatively small price to pay for an entrée that later can be parleyed into capital.

Another service making the rounds in banking is called anticipatory banking. "You look at the individual and consider his goals and what he is trying to accomplish," says one purveyor. "Only after receiving that feedback do we tell him what we think we can do for him."

Anticipatory banking does *not* offer the litany of products and services available through other programs. If you are married, anticipatory banks will treat you and your spouse as a team. Some banks assign two people to each account—a lending specialist and a deposit placement specialist. The rationale is that the financial environment has become too sophisticated and too complicated for any one banking officer to master it all.

If you don't have a bedrock foundation of capital reserves or if you have a fluctuating income, a line-of-credit arrangement might be suggested. Many no-frills customers, while high-income earners, have uneven cash flows, and they want or need to make purchases at times not matched by incoming cash. Responsive banks strive to take care of all these concerns up front. Officers and account managers in banks practicing an anticipatory approach to providing services may actively examine account portfolios and attempt to diagnose and project what the customer may need even before the customer may recognize it or even know about it.

Chapter 5: Hot Tips and Insights

✓ Too many entrepreneurs seek funds after they *have* to have them. To get over the reflexive tendency to ask for money too late in the game, consider that it takes at least three times longer to get a loan than most loan applicants contemplate when first identifying the need to get a loan in the first place.

✓ When seeking debt you will have to pinpoint how much money you need, over what period, how the funds will be used, and when and how you will pay the money back.

✓ Familiarize yourself with other available financing sources before walking into the bank.

✓ Obtaining a loan for the second time from a bank can be much more difficult than the first time. The irony of financing is that as revenues are increasing and the business is about to expand, it becomes most difficult to portray the business in a favorable light.

✓ Always select your bank carefully. Examine them just as closely as they examine you. Find out who is on the board, who their officers are, the size of their assets, and the reputation they have in the community. What do they charge compared to other banks; what types of programs are available; and what is their relationship to others in your line of business?

✓ Maintain a network of communications with peers and join those civic and community associations in which representatives from several banks are members.

✓ Never take your present bank for granted; they may let you down at any moment. This is not being defensive, just realistic.

✓ By cultivating a relationship in advance, you can request and possibly get lower interest rates than the going rate on loans, and have other service costs eliminated. The better the loan officer understands your business—the more information he has on you in his file—the more effectively you'll be represented to the bank loan committee.

✓ When it comes to actually negotiating the loan, start by whittling away at the extra fees.

✓ When you have a solid credit rating, things work in your favor. People whom you've not met before are ready to offer loans or do business with you.

✓ To obtain badly needed funds without appearing to have great need for them, make your request for financial assistance as part of an overall business planning process, and not because you have to have it or else.

✓ The strongest argument for lending money for a project is that it's a good project. Get others, such as your lawyer or accountant, to recommend you.

✓ Find out which credit bureaus your bank is using to get reports on you, and request your own copies. Then, if the report includes something you dispute, you can challenge it.

✓ Take advantage of new banking relationships and arrangements that are rapidly coming on line as the banking industry scrambles to keep pace with competitors, amidst new regulations in a rapidly changing society.

6

MINIMIZING YOUR RISK

There was a time when a fool and his money were
soon parted, but now it happens to everybody.

Adlai Stevenson

Everyday the chance exists for some disastrous event to occur,
one that could directly impact on your day-to-day operations,
affect profits, and result in serious financial losses. Just being in
business is a risky proposition. You've worked hard to get your
business where it is today. You probably manage a valuable group
of employees, conduct business with a growing roster of clients,
and may even own property.

Is your business adequately, but not overly, insured? Do you
know what kind of protection you need? Are you using employee
insurance benefits to their best advantage? Dollars spent on insurance you don't need is like paying the neighborhood racketeer
protection money—you will never reap the benefits.

Insurance coverage is one of those tedious topics most of us
would rather forget, and probably no area of business or consumer purchase is made with such haste and lack of forethought
as insurance. Yet, the odds favor that the typical company will
incur some type of loss, particularly at a crucial time for the
business. For example, one in four CEOs experience a disability
at some time or another and are taken away from the business
for weeks if not months.

Flood, fire, theft, and liability claims do occur. Never assume that a particular loss won't happen to you. Also, the nagging and rapidly rising costs of employee benefits, particularly health care and unemployment insurance, are enough to keep one awake at nights. For each employee, Federal and state unemployment insurance alone can annually cost from $700 to $1000 or more. The unforeseen, costly event has a way of rearing its ugly head when you're already down. You can't operate a viable business on the hope and prayer that nothing will go wrong—something will and it always has a cost.

To avoid predictable larger losses, it makes sense to incur smaller, regular losses in the form of insurance premiums or self-insurance. This chapter will highlight some of the key areas where you can save some dollars, but stay protected.

Shopping for an Agent.   If you have yet to find a qualified agent, start doing some research. Attend business workshops, ask for referrals from friends or business acquaintances, or consult with the variety of professional associations for a list of members or recommended insurance agents. According to Lee Little, a life underwriter based in Washington, D.C., "You can eliminate almost 90 percent of the field by seeking out an insurance agent who is a member of a respected professional association and can demonstrate five or more years of experience."

"Look for an agent who is a problem-finder as well as a problem-solver," adds Little. "What you don't need is a product-peddler." Here are two professional associations to help in your search:

National Association of Professional Insurance Agents
400 N. Washington Street
Alexandria, VA 22314
(703) 836-9340

Independent Insurance Agents of America
127 S. Peyton Street
Alexandria, VA 22314
(703) 683-4422

MINIMIZING LONG-TERM INSURANCE COSTS

If you're like most managers and want to maximize your future profits, comparing the various types of insurance coverage available to you can be very important. Insurance companies and the agents who represent them are under constant pressure to provide cost-competitive services and are continually designing or redesigning programs to meet the needs of growing businesses.

Here are some rules of thumb when examining insurance costs:

- Avoid duplication in insurance.
- Cover your largest loss exposure first.
- Buy coverage in as large a unit as possible, i.e., package plans.
- Periodically review your program even after purchasing and implementing it.
- Structure your coverage with as high a deductible as you can afford.

Ideally, you want to achieve a complete plan that fulfills your company's insurance objectives and is (1) clearly stated, (2) clearly assigned, (3) well-organized, and (4) well-recorded.

Minimizing Risks. Because your company is insured against possible loss does not mean that you don't have to worry about preventing it. Your preventive efforts alone may end up saving you hundreds of thousands of dollars! Before you invest in any insurance for your company, spend some time evaluating the ways in which your company could suffer a loss.

Unless you run a large corporation, you likely do not have a full-time risk manager on staff. Consequently, you or someone on your staff must adopt the additional responsibility of determining risk and minimizing exposure to it. Anytime you compare insurance programs, study their costs specifically as they relate to the possible risks you've outlined for your company.

The biggest problem with handling risk management yourself is that you may not be able to effectively analyze those things that may cause a loss for your company. You may also have limited ability to select the best way of dealing with each potential for loss. The key to a successful risk-management program, one that actually enables your company to reduce costs while remaining protected, is finding the right balance among the types of insurance necessary.

ESSENTIAL INSURANCE COVERAGE

Below is a checklist of essential insurance prepared by the Small Business Administration. By reviewing this checklist, you will be better able to identify, minimize, and eliminate certain risks for your company. You will have then taken a major step toward both safeguarding your company and pinpointing problem areas that require further action.

For all businesses there are four types of insurance that are essential: fire, liability, automobile, and workers' compensation insurance. Crime insurance, usually considered desirable coverage, is needed for certain businesses in certain locations.

Checklist of Essential Insurance

	No Action Needed	Look Into This
Fire Insurance		
1. Coverage for other perils—windstorm, hail, smoke, explosion, vandalism, and malicious mischief—can be added to your basic fire insurance for a relatively small additional sum.	___	___
2. For comprehensive coverage, you might consider one of the all-risk contracts that offer the broadest protection for the money.	___	___

Figure 6.1. *continued*

	No Action Needed	Look Into This

3. An insurance company may indemnify or, rather, compensate you for your losses in one of several ways: (1) payment of the actual cash value of the property at the time of loss; (2) repair or replacement of the property with similar material; (3) reimbursement of loss based on the agreed or appraised value of all the property. ———— ————

4. You are allowed to insure property you don't own, but you must have an insurable interest, i.e., financial, when a loss occurs. However, this is not required at the time the insurance contract is made. ———— ————

5. Upon sale of the property, you cannot pass along the insurance policy unless you have permission from the insurance company. ———— ————

6. In the case of several policies on your property, be aware that you can still collect only the amount of your actual cash loss because all the insurers share the payment proportionately. ———— ————

7. Special protection other than the standard fire insurance policy is required to cover the loss by fire of accounts, bills, currency, deeds, evidence of debt, money, and securities. ———— ————

8. If you have an insured building that is vacant or unoccupied for more than 60 consecutive days, coverage is suspended unless you have a special endorsement in your policy that cancels this provision. ———— ————

Figure 6.1. *continued*

	No Action Needed	Look into This

9. By concealing or misrepresenting any fact or circumstance to the insurer regarding your insurance or the interest of the insured, your policy may be voided—before or after a loss. ____ ____

10. An increase in the hazard of fire may cause your insurance company to suspend your coverage even for losses not caused by the increased hazard. (This could occur if, for instance, you rented part of your insured building to a cleaning company.) ____ ____

11. An insurance company will always expect you to use all available resources to protect your property from further loss following an actual loss. Otherwise, you risk having your coverage canceled. ____ ____

12. To receive compensation for your loss, you must furnish a complete inventory of all damaged, destroyed, and undamaged property within a specific time period (usually 60 days). This inventory should include details of quantities, costs, actual cash value, and amount of loss claimed. ____ ____

13. In the event of a disagreement between you and your insurer over the amount of a particular loss, a resolution may be reached through special appraisal procedures included in your fire insurance policy. ____ ____

14. Both you and your insurance company may cancel at any time. You may get part of your premium returned. The insurance company must provide a five-day written notice of cancellation. ____ ____

Figure 6.1. *continued*

	No Action Needed	Look into This

15. Remember the coinsurance clause that states you must carry insurance equal to 80 to 90 percent of the value of the insured property. If you accept this clause, you will get a substantial reduction in your premiums. ____ ____

16. When your loss is a direct result of a third party's negligence, your insurer has the right to sue this party for the amount it paid you for your loss. This is known as the insurer's right of subrogation and can be waived if necessary and upon the request of your agent to the insurer. ____ ____

17. Buildings that are under construction can also be insured for fire, lightning, extended coverage, vandalism, and malicious mischief. ____ ____

Liability

1. Legal liability limits of as much as $1 million are no longer considered excessive or unreasonable for small businesses. ____ ____

2. As required by your insurer, you should always notify your insurer immediately after any incident occurs on your property that might lead to a future claim, regardless of how unimportant the incident might seem. ____ ____

3. With specifically-stated insurance, most liability policies now cover personal injuries, i.e., libel, slander, etc., in addition to bodily injuries. ____ ____

4. Be aware that your business may even be subject to damage claims from trespassers. ____ ____

Figure 6.1. *continued*

	No Action Needed	Look into This

5. The exercise of "reasonable care" may still hold you legally liable for damages in some cases.   ____   ____

6. Whether or not the suit against you is false or fraudulent, your liability insurer pays court costs, legal fees, and interest on judgments, in addition to the liability judgments themselves.   ____   ____

7. You can be insured for liability due to the acts of others who are working under contracts you have with them.   ____   ____

8. If you are held liable for fire loss of the property of others in your care, you would normally not receive coverage from your fire or general liability insurance. This risk, rather, can be covered by fire legal liability insurance or through requesting subrogation waivers from the insurers of the owners of the propery.   ____   ____

Automobile Insurance

1. If you request an employee or subcontractor to use a car on your behalf, you can be legally liable even if you don't own the car.   ____   ____

2. Low-cost fleet policy generally insures five or more automobiles or motorcycles under one ownership that are operated as a fleet for business purposes. This protects against both material damage to your vehicles and liability to others for property damage or personal injury.   ____   ____

3. Deductibles are often available in almost any amount, such as $250 or $500, and can reduce your premiums.   ____   ____

Figure 6.1. *continued*

	No Action Needed	Look Into This

4. If you or your employee is involved in an automobile accident, automobile medical payments insurance pays for medical claims, including your own, regardless of possible negligence. ____ ____

5. While driving in most states, you must carry liability insurance or be prepared to provide other proof of financial responsibility, i.e., a surety bond, when you are involved in an accident. ____ ____

6. Uninsured motorist protection is available to cover your own bodily injury claims from someone who has no insurance. ____ ____

7. Any personal property stored in an automobile and not attached to it (for example, merchandise being delivered) is not covered under an automobile policy. ____ ____

Workers' Compensation

1. As an employer, federal and common law requires you to: (1) provide employees a safe place to work; (2) hire competent fellow employees; (3) provide safe tools; and (4) warn employees of any danger that may exist. ____ ____

2. If you fail to provide the conditions stated above, then you may be liable for damage suits brought by an employee and possible fines or prosecution. ____ ____

3. The various state laws set limits on the level or types of benefits payable under workers' compensation. ____ ____

4. Similarly, some employees may not be covered by workers' compensation laws as determined by the particular state. ____ ____

Figure 6.1. *continued*

	No Action Needed	Look Into This
5. In most states, you are legally bound to cover your employees under workers' compensation.	——	——
6. To save money on workers' compensation insurance, check to see that your employees are properly classified. (See the discussion later in this chapter on self-insurance for workers' compensation.)	——	——
7. Workers' compensation rates generally range from 0.1 percent of the payroll for "safe" occupations to approximately 25 percent or more of the payroll for very hazardous occupations.	——	——
8. By implementing safety and loss-prevention measures in your company, you will most likely reduce your accident rate to below the average and therefore reduce your workers' compensation premiums.	——	——

Figure 6.1.

PROPERTY LOSSES

Losses due to fire or other common perils, such as lightning, windstorm, or vandalism, fall under the general heading of "property losses." It's likely that you are *underinsured* in this area. Damage may affect only a small part of your company's property, leaving records and operations intact. However, the damage can also be the destruction of a building, leaving everything in your offices or plant unsalvageable.

Because property damage covers more than just damage to the building itself, it is wise to consider insurance for property damage to cover equipment, inventory, and business operations being brought to a halt. What would happen to your company's financial situation if a gas main break forced you to close business for one or more days?

Many companies today that are underinsured for property loss do not realize that the value of their real estate, whether owned or not, has likely increased significantly. Even without inflation and in the midst of soft real estate markets, property values nationally have risen dramatically, sometimes by as much as 200 or 300 percent over the last ten years.

Beware of Coinsurance Clauses.   Most property and casualty insurance policies contain a coinsurance clause written into the policy by the insurance company. This clause is inserted by the insurance company to safeguard itself in the event of a partial loss. It works like this: It lowers the amount paid to you, the insured, if you fail to maintain adequate coverage based on the replacement value of the property.

For example, if you have an $80,000 policy with an 80-percent coinsurance clause and your property is valued at $100,000, then you would receive full compensation in the event of a partial loss, if you maintained the policy for at least 80 percent of the value. If you didn't increase the amount of your policy and your property appreciated in value to $120,000, you would still only have an $80,000 policy with an 80-percent insurance clause.

If you filed a claim for $40,000, you wouldn't receive the full amount. Instead you would receive only $26,667, 67 percent of the total claim, because you insured only 67 percent of the minimum requirement ($80,000 divided by $120,000).

In short, the percentage you can collect on your loss will depend on what percent of the full value of the property you have insured it for. To avoid underinsurance of your company's property, consult with your casualty insurance agent to be sure your policy covers the current replacement value of your property.

EMPLOYEE BENEFIT COVERAGES

Insurance premiums to cover employee benefits can drain your funds fast. Yet you may have little leeway in tampering with employee expectations. Let's look at some of the biggest offenders and what can be done about them.

Group Life Insurance

Payment for group insurance premiums is deductible up to $50,000, while the benefit value is not taxable income to your employees. Hence offering a slightly lower salary but compensating with group life insurance is appealing to many employees. Affordable group coverage is available for groups of less than ten employees, with those employees paying part of the cost; yet, in all cases, 75 percent of the employees must elect to participate for you to qualify. If an employee leaves your company, he or she may convert group insurance to a private plan, without a medical exam, within 30 days after leaving the job.

"Split-dollar insurance," a cash-value life insurance policy in which two parties (usually employer and employee) share in paying the premium can often be used to buy inexpensive insurance for a valued employee. It can also be used as a deferred compensation plan, for coverage during retirement years, and to pay estate taxes.

With split-dollar insurance, the employer or the employee may own the policy. In the case of the former, "the endorsement method," the employer is the beneficiary of either the amount of the premiums it has paid or the policy's cash value, whichever is greater. The employee's beneficiary receives the balance.

In the case of the latter "collateral assignment method," the employer loans the amount of the annual increase in cash value or premium due to the employee, who then assigns the policy to the employer as collateral for the loans. If the employee dies, the employer receives a sum equal to the outstanding loans, and the balance of the insurance is paid to the employee's beneficiary.

While the disadvantages of split-dollar insurance for you as an employer include the necessity of a formal agreement and the unavailability of a tax deduction on premium outlays, it has several cash advantages. It is a low-cost investment; you can obtain the return of all premiums paid; you can borrow against the cash value; and the policy cash value itself can be treated as a corporate asset.

Health-Care Insurance

It's likely that you are overpaying for health-care insurance. When Montgomery Ward first offered group health insurance to its employees in 1912, it was hailed as a remarkable new innovation because it would supposedly expand access to medical care to millions of working Americans while not costing much. As the demand for health-care coverage increased over the years, so did health-care expenditures.

Numerous alternatives have been tried and introduced as a way of helping to stem the staggering rate of health-care insurance. You're probably familiar with many of them: HMOs, PPOs, IPAs, and EPOs. Yet, the average U.S. company's medical costs rose by almost 13.6 percent within this time frame, to about $2,600 per employee.

In fact, most managers will tell you that health-care costs rose almost twice as quickly as all other costs during the 1970s, and of late is struggling to keep pace with medical costs, which are rising by 20 to 23 percent per year. No solution presently exists for controlling health-care costs once and for all. Expensive medical technology will continue to be developed, new and costly treatments will take precedence over older, more affordable ones, and the United States population will continue to grow older. In the 1990s, health-care costs have exploded—following an impending national upheaval, a day of reckoning will surely come.

According to one consultant who specializes in the design and administration of health-insurance plans, small and medium-sized companies in particular are finding it difficult to find cost-effective solutions because insurance carriers are making up for heavy underwriting losses with annual rate increases of 35 to 50 percent. These staggering increases pose a real threat to small companies.

If you haven't carefully reviewed alternatives to your health-care costs, you could indeed be overinsuring. Yet, many executives and entrepreneurs regard managing health-care costs as unimportant compared to other aspects of doing business. The reality is that selecting and purchasing health-care insurance for yourself and your employees can be one of the most complex things you'll do in business. For your company's sake, don't delegate this responsibility to junior management or a benefits manager who does not have input from above.

Sometimes employees have strong attachments to their health-care plans that can render any company's efforts to contain costs a disaster. In one company last year, four out of five workers who quit their jobs did so because of moves to cut their health insurance. Any change in your company's health-care coverage must be done with great sensitivity. Here's a look at what some companies are doing about exorbitant health-care insurance costs.

Shifting Costs to Employees.   Among the alternatives developed by business in recent years is the shift of more health-care costs to employees. This includes transferring payment of health-care premiums to employees and even requiring fixed-sum payments toward health-care benefits.

Self-Insuring.   Companies are also eliminating insurance carriers, choosing instead to self-insure. Many companies are relying on prescribed standards for medical treatment in the hopes of eliminating lengthy hospital stays and unnecessary operations.

Partial Self-Insurance.   In addition to the increasingly popular concept of managed health care, in which a selected group of doctors and hospitals is assembled to deliver appropriate care, partial self-insurance, where a company assumes a greater share of the health insurance risk, is now gaining ground as an equally popular alternative for small businesses. Based upon the premise that companies retain a larger share of the health-care risk and the administrative responsibility, self-insurance, according to some experts, can lower costs without reducing benefit levels.

Partial self-insurance works best for firms with 25 or more employees. It involves a hybrid approach that combines the company's own funds with policies written by "reinsurers." Instead of paying a substantial premium to the health-insurance carrier for broad coverage, the company, for example, might retain the risk of catastrophic loss above the $10,000 individual limit.

The self-insuring company or "reinsurers" pick up where the traditional carrier's underlying premium leaves off. By assuming a limited risk, health-insurance premium rates can run at about 25 percent less than traditional premium rates. To prevent individual claims from reaching prohibitive levels, a company can also add another form of insurance to the policy known as "aggregate stop loss." This insurance establishes a limit on the total amount of individual claims a company is liable for. It costs about five percent of traditional health coverage.

You can cut up to 30 percent of your traditional health insurance premium by paying for catastrophic-loss and stop-loss coverage. Even after paying out all claims to your employees; you may have spent less for partial insurance than for regular health coverage because the traditional insurance company's profit is factored into what goes to the insured.

Other advantages of partial self-insurance include the ability for your company to design a plan that best suits your employees' needs, that is, you can set your own coverage maximums and deductibles. Your company can also benefit from placing its pool of funds for settling claims in an interest-earning account, rather than paying premiums to the insurance carrier.

While private insurance companies argue that self-insuring groups should stick to their own line of business, there is no economic justification for this. A benefits consultant who is not on commission can help determine how your company can take a more active role in providing health insurance.

Smoke-Free Environments, Lower Costs. More businesses are recognizing the value of providing a smoke-free environment for their workforce. Increasingly, particularly in suburban office parks and office town-house complexes, small clusters of employees can be seen standing outside, even in the cold, smoking. This is the telltale sign of a company that has instituted a smoke-free office environment. These companies will enjoy low absentee rates, higher productivity, and a decrease in their health-insurance costs.

Workers' Compensation

How can self-insurance be used to lower workers' compensation costs, a financial responsibility common among all businesses? High costs, while almost always blamed on insurance companies, are often the result of costs imposed on them by the state's eligibility and benefit requirements. Nevertheless, potential distortions and rigidities caused by administered pricing in the workers' compensation market have virtually eliminated the comparative advantage of private insurers.

The best alternative may currently be for groups of small businesses to insure against this burdensome responsibility—provided they can answer to all the required needs of injured workers. Usually, employers are responsible for paying all medical costs and indemnity benefits (usually a proportion of wages) in cases where workers become injured or ill as a result of on-the-job activity. Each state determines its own rules for paying injured or ill workers, and most require an employer to meet all benefits liabilities.

While workers' compensation coverage is readily available through a traditional carrier, smaller firms who recognize the inequities of conventional plans are writing their own coverage, or banding together to develop a workers' compensation product as a group. The reason for joining efforts is simple: The bigger the operation, the more the risk can be spread out.

To date, trade associations are the most active in group self-insured workers' compensation programs. Not surprisingly, their growing involvement has led to concern over how these groups should be treated by their states' respective insurance regulatory systems. After all, many of these associations are beginning to look and act like mutual insurance companies.

That's not your issue, however. Your goal is to identify those trade and professional associations or societies who offer such programs. If you are not already aware of the key associations in your field, two reference works will be of enormous aid: *Gale's Encyclopedia of Associations*, published by Gale Research Inc. out of Detroit, MI, is a four-volume set describing more than

22,000 active associations, organizations, clubs and other non-profit membership groups in every field of human endeavor. Volumes are arranged by national organizations of the United States, geographic and executive indexes, new associations and projects, and international organizations. Gale also provides two periodical issues of updated information for associations listed in volume one.

The second reference guide is the *National Trade Associations of the United States*, John J. Russell, managing editor. Published by Columbia Books in Washington, DC, this guide lists 7200 active national trade and professional associations and labor unions. Information includes the year founded, the name of the executive director, number of members, staff size, annual budget, historical notes, names of publications, and date, place, and expected attendance to the annual meeting.

In addition, a third reference guide may come in handy: the *National Directory of Addresses and Telephone Numbers*, published by General Information Inc, of Bothell, WA. It contains 66,000 alphabetical listings, with complete addresses and zip codes, of the biggest and most influential organizations in the United States, including all major businesses, *insurance agencies*, government agencies, hospitals, and associations. It also contains 35,000 fax numbers and 9,400 toll-free numbers— 210,000 listings in all.

An Intriguing Idea.   If the idea of self-insuring to cover workers' claims is intriguing to you, particularly to handle some of the employee-related coverages, here's a review of the basic prerequisites. All insurers must meet state obligations for insuring injured workers, including providing substantial equity and long-run efficiency. Your state officials will want to know about your administrative arrangements, including issues such as membership eligibility, managerial qualifications, subcontractors' financial obligations, and the liability of members who make judgments against their associates.

You'll also have to exhibit strong financial footing, including a minimum net worth, the ability to contribute to your fund, and the ability to maintain excess insurance requirements and reserve requirements for losses. In safeguarding your funds, you also will be restricted to a range of allowable investments. Nevertheless, as the issue continues to be discussed, group self-insurance for workers' compensation will certainly continue to grow in popularity.

Disability Insurance.   In addition to workers' compensation insurance, you can purchase insurance to cover the lost income of workers who suffer a short- or long-term disability that is not related to your company. Again, you could seek to more than offset the cost of providing this benefit by offering lower wages. In the case of permanent disability, you can get lifetime income coverage for your employees.

Key-Man Insurance.   If your company relies upon one or more key employees, you may want to provide key-employee life and disability insurance, owned by and payable to your company, to protect your company from the loss of a key employee's input. In a small business, the existence of this policy can be the make-or-break factor when an essential employee is not available. While proceeds of key-employee policies are not subject to income tax, premiums are not a deductible business expense.

Retirement Income.   Under the Employees Retirement Income Security Act (ERISA), you can get an income tax deduction for funds used for your and your employees' retirement if you are self-employed. Annuities, which guarantee retirement income for life, can be fixed or variable and need to be analyzed with respect to inflation.

OTHER INSURANCE YOU MAY WANT

There remain some types of insurance that, while not entirely essential, can add significantly to the security and well-being of your business. They include: business interruption insurance, crime insurance, glass insurance, and rent insurance. To establish your company's particular need for one or all of these desired coverages, review the following points and discuss the issues with your insurance agent.

Business Interruption Insurance.   This can include insurance to cover fixed expenses that would have to continue even if a fire closed down your business, that is, salaries for key employees, taxes, interest, depreciation, and utilities, as well as the profits you would lose. With properly written contingent business interruption insurance, you can also collect if your business is interrupted by the halted operations of a supplier or customer due to fire or other perils.

A business interruption policy can provide payments to you for the amount you spend in facilitating the reopening of your business after a fire or other perils. When a peril seriously disrupts your business but does not actually force its closing, coverage for the extra expenses you incur is available. In addition, if you lack power, light, heat, gas, or water normally furnished by your public utility company, you can get business interruption insurance to indemnify you.

Crime Insurance.   Burglary insurance excludes certain property such as fur articles in a showcase window and manuscripts. To secure coverage for money in a safe, inventoried merchandise, or damage caused during the course of a burglary, you must make a written addition to your burglary insurance policy. In all cases, coverage is granted only when there is visible evidence of a burglar's forced entry.

Robbery insurance can protect you and your company from loss of property, money, and securities by force, trickery, or threat of violence on or off your premises. If your company is required to make frequent deliveries of merchandise, you may want to discuss this further with your agent. Crime policies can be tailored to meet your needs. It can cover other types of loss by theft, destruction, and disappearance of money and securities in addition to those losses incurred in the course of a burglary or robbery. You can even obtain coverage for employee theft (more on employee theft in Chapter 10).

If your company is located in a high-risk area and cannot get insurance through conventional channels without paying exorbitant rates, consult your agent or state insurance commissioner for information on the Federal crime insurance plan.

Rent Insurance.   This insurance is available to cover your company's rent payments in the event a particular property becomes unusable due to fire or other insured perils and your lease requires continued rent payments. If you or your company serves as landlord of the property, you can also insure against loss suffered when the lease is canceled because of fire, and you must relet the property at a reduced rate.

   Certainly, insurance is not your favorite topic. When you know you're adequately protected, however, and are using insurance benefits to your favor, insurance is not such a demon.

Chapter 6: Hot Tips and Insights

✔ The odds favor that you will incur some type of loss, particularly at a crucial time for the business. One in four CEOs experience a significant disability. Flood, fire, theft, and liability claims do occur. Never assume that a particular loss won't happen to you.

✔ To avoid predictable larger losses, it makes sense to incur smaller, regular losses in the form of insurance premiums or self-insurance.

✔ Seek an insurance agent who is a member of a respected professional association and can demonstrate five or more years of experience. Look for an agent who is a problem-finder as well as a problem-solver.

✔ Rules of thumb when examining insurance costs: avoid duplication in insurance; cover your largest loss exposure first; buy coverage in as large a unit as possible and review your program even after purchase; pay as high a deductible as you can afford.

✔ The best plan is one that fulfills your company's insurance objectives and is clearly stated, clearly assigned, well-organized, and well-recorded.

✓ Before investing in any insurance for your company, evaluate the ways in which your company can suffer a loss.

✓ It's likely that you are underinsured for potential losses due to fire or other common perils, such as lightning, windstorm, or vandalism, which fall under the general heading of "property losses."

✓ More businesses are attempting to shift more health-care costs to employees, including transferring payment of health-care premiums to employees and requiring fixed-sum payments toward health-care benefits.

✓ Also explore eliminating insurance carriers, through self-insurance or partial self-insurance, where a company assumes a greater share of the health-insurance risk.

✓ Cut up to 30 percent of your traditional health-insurance premium by paying for catastrophic-loss and stop-loss coverage.

✓ Offer a smoke-free environment to enjoy lower absentee rates, higher productivity, and a decrease in employee health-insurance costs.

✓ Identify those trade or professional associations or societies who offer group insurance programs.

✓ In addition to workers' compensation insurance, you can purchase insurance to cover the lost income of workers who suffer a short- or long-term disability that is not related to your company.

✓ If your company relies upon one or more key employees, you may want to provide key-employee life and disability insurance, owned by and payable to your company, to protect your company from the loss of a key employee's input.

7

COLLECTING YOUR CASH

In touching money we touch the keystone of character.

John Ruskin

It's easy to get upset about the money others owe you, until you acknowledge that you have to train customers how and when to pay you. Most businesses either have a coordinated policy in place and make an effort to be paid promptly or have adopted a less-than-adequate approach to collecting what you've earned.

Have you noticed how many doctors and dentists have adopted a policy of asking you to pay *right now*, on your way out the door? Have you considered how many new opportunities there are to use your major credit card at places that aren't even oriented toward retail sales, from the pledge you make during a public television fund raiser to the prepaid popcorn you order to help a local service organization?

There is a good reason for immediate payment and credit card use. For most businesses collecting payment is a difficult, time-consuming activity that often costs companies more money than the actual amount owed by the customer. In fact, collecting debts has become a large enough problem to merit its own industry. Consider the collection departments of sizable stores and companies, independent collection agencies, and accountants and lawyers who specialize in collection problems and litigation.

Nationally, delinquent accounts turned over to collection

agencies total more than $20 billion per year, with an estimated additional $20 billion that businesses simply eat as bad debt. The collection industry estimates that between three and five percent of consumer debts and two and four percent of commercial debts go bad. Unfortunately, some businesses become so mired in debt and collection problems that they must close their doors for good.

The paradox for businesses faced with collection problems is that the time never seems to be right to ask for payment. If things are going well otherwise, it's easy enough to overlook a few slow or nonpayers. If things are going badly who wants to devote an inordinate amount of time to a task hardly anyone finds enjoyable?

THE MYTH OF COLLECTING RECEIVABLES

While collecting your cash *is* important, you don't want to become shortsighted as to what *sustains* a positive cash flow. Too many managers and entrepreneurs still believe that a few simple principles govern one's ability to maintain a positive cash flow. They are deluded by textbooks that promise that if you collect the proportion of money you've earned first, and take time to collect the money you've committed to expenses, your cash flow will surely runneth over, and you will dwell in the house of the restored forever more.

This is hogwash. As we've discussed in earlier chapters, your payroll may be high or you may be getting so little productivity out of your staff that if all your customers paid in dollar bills on the spot, you'd still be strapped for cash.

Your purchasing policies may be suspect in that your cost of goods sold or operating expenses and supplies are so out of line compared to norms in your industry that you couldn't have a positive cash flow if you tripled your sales and had no accounts payable. It may also be that your phone and utility expenses and insurance and benefits programs may be eating you alive.

If you're sloppy with check-handling procedures and have poor internal controls, in addition to poor collections, you may experience shrinkage in excess of last month's earnings. If you're inept at submitting bids and proposals, or are a dreamer when it comes to preparing revenue projections, your cash forecast will be gloomy.

As we saw in Chapter 5, if you haven't made the right contacts with people who can fork over large sums to help you finance legitimate growth, you may carry your upturned hat in hand into a bank some morning and end up begging a stranger to bail you out.

> Don't ever believe that collecting quickly and paying slowly is all it takes for a healthy cash flow.

Collecting quickly is *usually* to your advantage; there are exceptions, however. It's not wise to offend a possibly lucrative, long-term customer because of injudicious collection efforts. It is also bad business when industry norms and customer expectations call for an entirely different approach. Can you imagine trying to collect from a widow the day after the funeral?

Depending on your type of business, and regardless of the steps you've taken to ensure that payments are made on time, you're bound to face at least some problems with uncollected debts. As we'll discuss, to protect yourself, know thy customer. The more you know or can assemble about each customer, the more tools you have to collect.

A DOLLAR EARNED IS NOT A DOLLAR COLLECTED

Two women started a graphics and advertising communications firm in Colorado called HKL Communications. This was the first such firm in their small but growing city. They marketed their services by word of mouth only, since it was a particularly effective method and kept marketing costs at a minimum. One of their early clients traded them office space for retainer services.

With little capital investment, they were able to fill a service vacuum with no competition. Things were rosy indeed. HKL Communications soon grew to four full-time staffers, several part-time employees and a healthy roster of contractors who could be called upon as needed.

The client list grew. In addition to numerous local clients—from the merchants at the largest shopping mall in town to the one theatre in town—the firm managed to attract business from some national companies based in nearby Boulder. Traditionally, graphics and advertising is not a service area where one asks for payment "up front" or as a client is walking out the door. Rather, contracts are signed that include payment schedules, usually as timelines are met.

HKL Communications dutifully sent invoices as these segments were completed, causing the partner in charge of the bookkeeping to comment, "Just keeping track of invoices and sending them out on time was enough of a headache, especially since we were at a volume that was just too small to justify computerizing. When customers didn't pay and had to be re-invoiced and phoned, things got really crazy. I didn't want, and couldn't afford, to work nearly full-time chasing down bad accounts; but that's what was happening."

Two years into the business, the region's economy went into a tailspin. As money became tight, debtors became slow to pay. Some clients filed for bankruptcy and never paid HKL (or any other creditors). Others paid their other creditors first, knowing that HKL would never spend the money or time to "really go after" them. Debtors chose to pay suppliers, lawyers, and banks, well ahead of a graphics firm.

"The cash-flow problem was our downfall," explains a HKL partner about the firm's decision to close its doors after three years. "Oddly enough, we had plenty of clients. We just didn't have much in the way of reliable businesses that would pay our bills in a reasonable amount of time.

"About 15 percent of our clients paid promptly and about 25 percent paid after a second or third invoice," he explained. "But 60 percent either never paid or paid only after we'd spent so much time invoicing and calling that it was barely worth it."

It's a truism of business that the slower paying an account becomes, the more difficult it is to collect (see Table 7.1).

Collection Difficulties Over Time	
Time Overdue	Proportion Collectible
Over 60 days	89%
Over 6 months	67%
Over 12 months	45%
Over 24 months	23%
Over 36 months	15%
Over 5 years	Forget it!

Table 7.1.

EXTENDING CREDIT

Certainly, if you can collect payment in full upon making a sale, you will eliminate some causes of cash-flow problems. Managers who neither have to spend time tracking accounts receivable nor chase after late-paying or nonpaying customers are ahead of the game. If you're in a business, though, where it's commonplace to extend credit, you'll need to take action to ensure that your customers are current in their payments.

Assuming that you do extend credit, you'll want to get your hands on at least a portion of the fee or charge right away. One of the easiest ways to get cash flowing immediately into your business is to require a deposit or to establish a policy of progress payments. Some management consultants, for example, require one third of the estimated fee at the start of a project, another third at some agreed-upon midpoint, and the final third upon completion. You could lose a few clients this way, but you'll avoid having to make rigorous collection efforts. This policy also helps you steer clear of nonpaying clients before devoting a substantial amount of time, effort, and expense to a project.

Today, you have more options for encouraging speedy payment. You can always fax the invoices to avoid mail delays. If you work on a retainer basis, you can arrange to have clients transfer your monthly fee into your business account via electronic funds transfer. In general, to speed up payment of the outstanding balances, adopt the following policies:

1. Send out your invoices right away. Waiting until the end of the month to send out all your invoices might save you a little effort, but it can create cash-flow problems and "timing gaps," and cost you money in the process. If you delay sending out a bill of, say, $6,000 for two weeks (and consequently receive payment two weeks later than otherwise), you've lost about $14 in interest, based on an annual rate of 5.5 percent. Multiply that amount by 10 bills, and you've lost $140. Over a year's time, you've sacrificed more than $3,000 in lost interest income. Beyond that, however, you've lost the *opportunity* to use that money while you're waiting for it.

2. Reward prompt payers with an "early bird" discount. True, you'll lose a bit of income but you'll have more cash in hand to avoid cash-flow problems. (Chapter 3 discussed discounts, from the perspective of you as customer.)

3. Levy a surcharge on late payers. The flip side to the early bird discount is a surcharge on clients whose bills are outstanding beyond the agreed-upon terms. If, for example, payment is net 30, charge 1 or 1.5 percent per month on the outstanding balance. This encourages your customers to pay on time and enables you to recoup the money you've lost when carrying slow payers.

CONSUMERS' BAD DEBTS

A basic means of controlling bad debt is the credit application. Get the customer's home *and* business address, social security number, bank account numbers, and credit references—and keep the application current, updating it periodically for your old accounts. Experts suggest that the application include a clause which spells out that in the event the account becomes past due, the customer will pay collection and court costs. To make this enforceable, include specific terms regarding late payment fees on the application.

Retail businesses that seem like "cash-on-the-barrel-head" types, from restaurants to dry cleaners, are not immune to similar collection problems suffered by other types of businesses. Hundreds of hours can be eaten up by trying to collect on bad checks, personal lines of credit, or even credit card companies.

Nevertheless, an easy and convenient method for verifying if a check is likely to clear is to call the bank on which the check funds will be drawn. Offer your name, phone number, and detailed information from the check itself, including amount, account number, date, branch, check number, etc. While banks will not tell you specifically how much your customer has on account, they will tell whether or not the check will clear as of the present balance in the account at the time of call, less any amounts on hold.

You could be told, for example, that as of your call, the check will clear, only to have it not clear because other parties submitted claims on the funds ahead of yours. Still, the ability to simply call the bank and get an instant report is a resource worth tapping. In the event of a bad check, coupled with the customers noncooperation to pay, in many states you can now sue for additional damages and legal costs.

For retailers handling a volume of purchases made by personal check or credit card, a variety of verification services are readily available, each taking a small cut of sale.

HANDLING CUSTOMER CHECKS

All types of businesses, especially retailers, frequently have to deal with the problem of bad checks (and the related problem of stolen credit-card charges). Now high-tech point-of-sale verification systems that verify checking-account and credit-card numbers are available. Not far off is the widespread introduction of authorization services that offer money-back guarantees on any checks that are validated by preapproved point-of-sale verification systems and later returned by a bank.

No time-consuming off-site telephone calls are necessary to authorize purchases using available technology. These "on-line" type of systems provides merchants with instant verifications of both check and credit-card purchases, relieving the business owner of bad check risks and collection hassle headaches.

Why are point-of-sale verification systems becoming more important to business? A recent Payment Systems Education Association survey found that 72 percent of consumers *prefer* to pay by check.

Protection from Business Accounts. If a business account offers you a check, and days after you deposit it, it bounces, you have a number of built-in protections. First, keep in mind that any check that you receive, whether cashable or not, is prima facie evidence of debt. It's useful to know this because if your collection problem is not readily resolved, you can use this information to induce resolution, or take the rubber check writer to court.

In all states covered under the Uniform Commercial Code (Louisiana alone is *not* covered), if you receive a returned corporate check that does not identify the title of the signing party, you bring suit against that individual as well as the company. This keeps a lot of in-house accountants from signing a check when they have reason to believe it won't clear.

It's also useful to remind the bouncer that there are both civil and criminal penalties for passing bad checks.

IT'S MORE THAN TIME AND MONEY

For businesses that offer business-to-business services or who generate revenue based on contracts, collecting what's due can become a little sticky, if not downright aggravating. As if time and lost revenue collection difficulties aren't bad enough, additional problems occur when payments are consistently late or altogether uncollectible. Several of these are discussed below.

Added Interest Expense. When you are not able to collect on accounts due, you may need to borrow, or borrow more than originally anticipated, to maintain business as usual, thereby incurring added interest expense. Also, these borrowed funds were probably not factored into your early estimates of the capital needed to get into and stay in business.

Debts.   When cash flow slows to a trickle because of collection difficulties, one unhappy answer is to slow down payments to your own suppliers and creditors. This means mounting debts. Disgruntled creditors will write and phone you and levy late charges. Some may even cut off your credit. Yet, you need them.

Tied-up Capital.   Even if you have the capital to keep out of debt, and can avoid borrowing when collection problems arise, supporting slow collections is always a poor use of business capital. How much more profitable it would be if you could put that capital to work in a way that enhances the business rather than simply keeping it alive.

Bookkeeping Problems.   The more you have to invoice, reinvoice, and wait for payments, the more complex your bookkeeping becomes. Revenues and expenses don't readily balance, and projections for the future become entangled. You may even have to hire additional bookkeeping help, another unanticipated expense.

Borrowing Difficulties.   When your accounts show a substantial amount in "collectibles," with little real knowledge of when, or whether, collections can be made, potential lenders become skeptical. That loan application you had counted on for expansion or equipment may suddenly be rejected.

Competition.   All of these difficulties offer a good opening for the competition, new or old, in your market. Suddenly your business, which began with so much real promise, seems stuck in its tracks. You find yourself with little capital left for marketing or growing to capture the competitive edge.

WHO GETS CREDIT?

To better understand how you can more safely give credit to others, review the section "What Credit Bureaus Look For," presented in Chapter 5, which reveals how the credit bureaus assess a firm's credit-worthiness. Then, apply that same scrutiny with your customers.

The Credit-Worthiness of Your Customers. If you deal business-to-business, many collection problems can be avoided if you are willing to pay the cost of obtaining current credit reports. For a large fee, you can subscribe to commercial credit rating services that can supply detailed data about your customers.

With consumers, you can obtain credit histories from consumer credit bureaus such as TRW, CBI (Equifax). This is the preferred way to give credit only to the most credit-worthy (and demand cash from others). Unfortunately, this isn't feasible for many new or small businesses. Typically, a new or small business is happy to get new clients or customers and is not in a position to risk losing them by demanding cash until they prove themselves worthy of credit. Also, asking for cash payments may not work or may not be the way business is done in many circumstances.

SELF-INITIATED CREDIT CHECKS

Self-initiated credit checks are one way that many businesses approach the question of who gets credit, but these present their own problems. First, credit checks require a substantial investment in time and energy. Second, they require expertise in interpreting the meaning of the facts you uncover about someone's seeming ability to pay.

If you can obtain a report from a credit bureau or bank, you still may lack the information you need. A clean credit report simply means that the individual or firm in question generally pays. It doesn't mean that payment comes as quickly as you would like. And, of course, there are no guarantees. Many firms maintain good credit ratings up until the last day before bankruptcy, which may be the day your invoices arrive on their desks.

If you do decide to check on credit, you'll need to educate yourself on what to ask. Your bank may be able to get information from a potential customer's bank, or you may have to get it yourself. The answers to any of the following questions will be helpful:

- How long has the customer had an account?
- What is the average balance of the account?
- What is the customer's credit rating with the bank?
- Does the customer have a loan?
- Is the loan secured? What kind of security?
- When is the loan due?

You can't be certain of getting all the answers. Often, you'll get general, ballpark figures rather than specifics. Further complicating the situation, many firms or individuals whose credit you might check do not keep all their financial matters within one, or even two, institutions. They may have several different accounts and loans with different banks.

It never hurts to ask directly for three or more credit references. This affords quick, verifiable information and can enhance other information you've gathered. If you check credit through the client company itself, you may or may not get accurate answers to questions. However, the answers to any of them will help to assess a business:

- What is the corporate structure?
- Who are the principals of the company?
- What is the business experience of the principals?
- How long has the company been in this business?
- Who else gives them credit?
- What are the company's total assets?
- What are projected revenues?
- What has been the track record in recent years?

When extending credit, you are not unlike a bank offering a loan. You need to know whether there is a reasonable expectation that you will be paid fully and promptly. Unlike a bank loan department, however, you probably don't have the staff and expertise to fully investigate the situation and assure yourself real guarantees. In other words, checking credit is fine, but it is not a foolproof way to protect against collection problems.

A TOUGH PROBLEM FOR CONTRACTORS

Some large contracts or lengthy projects call for receipt of payment only upon completion, or at least upon completion of specific segments (more in Chapter 9). Within consumer markets, however, obtaining advanced payment can be difficult if not out of the question.

Suppose you hired a new construction firm to build an addition to your house and the company wanted substantial payment up front or when they had barely started foundation work. You might wonder about the firm's ability to deliver if it couldn't begin work before payment. Second, you might wonder how you could protect yourself against unsatisfactory work if you had already made payment. New firms need to establish good will, and often that means risking collection problems.

When Philip Masters, a South Carolina contractor, started his own construction firm, he began by taking on contracts with no progress payments. He had assembled a crew of laborers and craftsmen that he needed to keep busy. The fastest and easiest way to obtain construction contracts—on a signature and a promise—seemed to be the solution.

"I went through my start-up capital within a few months, paying my men and buying materials," he reported. He managed to delay some construction starts until clients made initial payments that would allow him to purchase materials. "I reasoned that at least I wouldn't be 'out-of-pocket' with the lumber and concrete companies."

When collections, which could average six to eight months, still presented problems, Masters began a policy of working only for customers he knew or who came highly recommended. However, that didn't hasten overall collections either.

"It's unbelievable, but you can't even count on friends and associates to come through with their payments. You can bump into them at a party or in the street, and they don't even bat an eye about the fact that they owe you thousands of dollars. What's worse is that you feel like such a dog for badgering friends for money they owe you."

Now before construction begins, Masters factors in materials, wages, and some profit when seeking partial payment. He alerts clients that payments will be due at specific points along the way. "And I still have problems collecting," he says.

"Sure, I could stop construction, but that would be cutting off my nose to spite my face. I'm in business to build, and I need to keep the men building if I ever hope to make a go of it. I think the only people that can really get around this slow-payment problem are those that have so much money behind them when they start a business, that they really don't need to be running a business at all!"

Masters may be exaggerating the costs of getting into business, but he is not overestimating the frustration of collections and the need to anticipate collection problems as a real cost of doing business. For many businesses, failure to realistically calculate these costs can be as serious as underestimating the cost of start-up inventory, taxes, and payroll.

LATE AND GETTING LATER—COLLECTION MISERIES

Going after deadbeat accounts necessitates a great deal of assertiveness and, understandably, is probably unpleasant for you. It often means letters, phone calls, thinly veiled threats, and personal visits. It means a lot of frustration and plenty of dead ends. If you give up, you don't get paid. If you hang on, you spend a lot of time trying to collect, and you irritate those who hate to see you coming. There is no easy way, but here's a system that has worked for many entrepreneurs.

In general, the collection route tends to break down into three chronological stages:

- Initial agreements
- Polite reminders
- Aggressive strategies

Initial Agreements.   Depending on the product or service in question, it may be possible, although time-consuming, to work out initial agreements about payment terms before work starts. These usually entail some mutually agreeable payment schedule and can be developed regardless of the size or importance of the customer. They can be particularly useful for customers who have a poor track record of payments.

One problem is that a customer who is slow to pay for work or goods delivered is likely to be just as slow to pay for various parts of the work or goods during the life of the agreement. Consequently, you are in a position of "trying to collect" for a single segment. Your leverage is that the customer may want to see the finished work or product badly enough to make segmented payments in a timely manner.

Although the initial agreement may also carry a deadline for final payment (e.g., 30 days after completion), don't expect to be immune from delays and excuses.

Such agreements are generally negotiated agreements, and it takes skill to negotiate terms that are mutually agreeable to all parties. Documenting the agreement by letter or formal contract is up to you.

Polite Reminders.   Polite reminders generally start with follow-up letters and are usually seen as a midpoint in the collection chronology. Here you'll need to set up a system for reminding yourself to send the reminder letters. Simple spread-sheet, accounting, or calendar software aids enormously in tracking who owes what and when they need to receive another reminder.

Your notices are most effective when they're sent directly to the department and preferably to the correct individual in the company from which you wish to collect. This person is probably *not* the individual or department you initially had contact with, so you will need to research the situation (see the section on phone calls below).

Effective collection letters are much more than a copy of the original invoice with "Payment Overdue" stamped on it. They work best when they contain specific information about the agreement, order or contract for which payment is due, including:

- A description of the goods or services involved
- Detail regarding completion date and first invoice
- Detail regarding any related written or oral agreements
- A reply envelope

Many champion bill collectors have found it useful to add a personal, narrative letter with the collection letter. The personal letter appeals to the customer's sense of fair play, reputation, or self-interest. Such narratives may require increasing assertiveness as accounts overdue linger on without any attempt at resolution. After you've written a couple of these and saved them on disk, simply change the particulars and reuse the letters with new deadbeats. A sample personalized collection letter is shown in Figure 7.1.

Polite, written reminders may also be more effective if they

Sample Personalized Collection Letter

Dear Bob Anderson,

I'm writing about the invoice for $1800 we submitted to you on February 12th for the six cartons of widgets you ordered. Eleven weeks have passed since you received shipment, and frankly, I'm concerned—I haven't heard from you and haven't been able to get a return phone call.

I don't have the financial capability or desire to finance aging receivables. Like you, I've got a payroll to meet, considerable overhead expenses, and a host of other expenses. I know you want to make good on your financial obligations—we certainly hope to continue to be your widget supplier.

I'd like to request payment in full at this time, or, if that's not possible, 50% payment and a call or note from you indicating when you will send the balance. I think my request is fair and know that you understand and appreciate our situation.

Here's to a great spring . . . look forward to hearing from you. Yours truly,

---

Figure 7.1.

are hand-carried by messenger, with signed receipt, or mailed with return receipt requested. This costs a little more, but offers a firm signal to the customer that you are serious.

Phone Calls Also Can Be Polite Reminders.   While you may anticipate the phone as a relatively quick and effective way to get attention for overdue accounts, when you actually begin making phone calls for collection purposes, you'll discover it is not so easy.

Typically, you'll make a number of calls before you find anyone who knows about the account. Often that individual isn't the person with authority to actually pay the account. Or the person with whom you speak may be very well-schooled in the "check-is-in-the-mail" runaround. His or her easiest tactic may be to agree, apologize profusely, get you off the phone and, ultimately, do nothing. Then, you wait for payment and start all over with more calls and letters.

The fax machine can be used in the collection process, if you keep the messages polite. If you know that the fax on the receiving end is in a "public" location, however, carefully consider whether using a fax reminder is appropriate for the situation, client, and sum in question. We know several entrepreneurs who relish the opportunity to uses faxes to greet and remind deadbeats first thing in the morning. "The heck with your privacy; give me my money."

Too many entrepreneurs are very conscientious in pleasing clients—even clients who are beginning to look like terminal deadbeats.

Aggressive Strategies.   When accounts become overdue for long periods, say over 90 days, you may want to resort to aggressive collection strategies. These are expensive, involving collection agencies and/or lawyers, and they often mean losing customers or clients who feel you are being difficult and heavy-handed.

Aggressive collection strategies become a must for most entrepreneurs. You will need to be armed with capital and resources to undertake them. Today, collection agencies, attorneys, and court costs are part of the predictable cost of being in business.

If you decide to retain a collection agency, first recognize that it can take up a great deal of your time, and if you're particularly persuasive, it may not be any more effective than you could be. There are many mediocre and poor collection agencies; you'll need to find a good one. Ask for referrals from others in business and your banker, accountant, or attorney. Also ask Small Business Administration Officials or your local Chamber of Commerce.

Ask collection agencies themselves for letters from satisfied clients or, barring that, names and phone numbers of satisfied clients. Then call the clients.

If you're satisfied with the referrals, turn one or two accounts over to the agency. If you're pleased with the results, try more. Avoid turning over dozens of clients; you need to get a feel for how the agency operates and how effective it is.

These days many accountants and attorneys will undertake collection efforts for you. Attorneys have even developed a "collections practice" to seek out delinquent customers. Quite often customers fearing judicial action pay their bills promptly over to the attorney. You are then notified that payment has been received and the attorney collects a transaction fee for his efforts. Whomever you may use, check out the company's policies and operations:

- Do they charge a flat fee (generally 50%)? It is better to use an agency that charges on a sliding scale, typically 33 to 50 percent, with the upper ranges for older and smaller accounts that are harder to collect.

- Do they demand a minimum fee if nothing is collected? If so, they may not work very hard to collect on small overdue payments, etc.

- Do they hold partial payments until the account due is paid in full? Partial payments should be treated with the same percentage split between you and the collection agency as with full payment.

- What methods do they use? If they bully and harass, your reputation may be at stake. If they simply make a few phone calls, you could have done that.

Using a collection agency doesn't mean you can forget about the account and go back to work. After all, just like your overdue customers, it has to set priorities, and your collection may not be at the top of its list. You'll also want to track your collection agency's success rate. If you feel that it is not working hard enough, you may be better off on your own.

SEGMENTING YOUR COLLECTIONS

Overlaying the three-step system introduced above is the process of segmenting your collections according to how you feel about the customer or client, and approaching them accordingly. Here's how it works:

With Kid Gloves. Clients who get the kid-glove treatment are those who, other than the sum outstanding, represent long-term, viable clients who can reward you with more profitable business and/or referrals. With this group, you proceed slowly, carefully, and definitely politely. You treat the outstanding sum as if it were simply an oversight and as if it represents no big deal to your business, although you would like to "bring the account up to date," or get the outstanding sum "off the books."

With Shuttle Diplomacy. This approach is reserved for those slow payers who just miss the cut for the Kid Gloves Approach. You're not sure if they represent more business or will provide good word of mouth. They are not contentious, however, and there is no need of jeopardizing your relationship with them. You simply like to conduct your business efficiently, including receiving payment in a timely manner.

With Boxing Gloves. You put on these gloves when there's little chance of repeat business, and you wouldn't want it anyway. With these holdouts you make contact frequently and forcefully, though remaining professional. Your objective is clear and your message is clear—to get your money. Here you use a wide variety of tools, including mail, phone, and fax, in a swift flurry of punches. If necessary, you are willing to become an irritant, though a professional one.

With the Swat Team. You use swat team techniques when boxing gloves don't work. The business relationship with these customers means absolutely nothing to you. It's your money and they're holding it. All weapons in your collection arsenal are assembled and lined up at the border. These include lawyers, hint of law suit, and collection agencies. You let the deadbeat know that you will never let up, the psychology being that it becomes less "painful" for them to pay you than to continue to be subject to your controlled, but intense effort to get your money. You may even contact the person by phone telling him you will personally collect payment. More often than not the customer will make up an excuse about being too busy or going out of town. Press the issue and settle on a time to meet. If the customer does not have enough money at the time ask him to post date the check with the date his checking account will have sufficient funds. If the check bounces you should consider two courses of action:

1. demand certified funds to replace the check drawn against "insufficient funds."
2. while you await arrangement on certified funds, call the bank the next day and thereafter to find out if funds are available for the check.

GOING THROUGH THE LEGAL SYSTEM

As you escalate your attempts to collect, you may need to retain an attorney to advise you of how far you can go and to keep you from overstepping the law. Accounts that remain uncollectible make everyone angry. It's tempting to go too far in terms of threats and harassment. Be careful—the cost of collecting can exceed the payment due.

Here are typical ways that entrepreneurs who extend credit can find themselves in the midst of legal hassles:

- Bringing suits for reasons other than collecting. A suit that is primarily for revenge and punishment is not a legal proceeding.
- Using overly aggressive collectors. Collectors who overstep their bounds leave the creditor wide open to legal action.
- Filing criminal charges when the debt itself is in dispute. Make sure it is clear that there really is payment owed to you.
- Using force in repossessions.
- Invading the debtor's right of privacy in making attempts to get payment.
- Using threats that may be interpreted as extortion or as blackmail.
- Publicly slandering the individual or company that is overdue with its payments.

When Paul Harrison began his surgical equipment manufacturing and sales firm in Columbus, he started with a handshake and a promise from customers. Later, when he had problems collecting on sales contracts, it became apparent that members of his sales force were being too "friendly" about verbal payment promises. They wanted the sales commissions, so they promised easy payment plans to the clients upon whom they called. Harrison changed that by sending them out with formal documents that constituted written payment agreements.

Still, many payments were painfully slow and were made only after considerable time was spent in writing letters and phoning. Harrison found himself busy meeting with sales personnel to assess problems, training them in spotting potential nonpayers ahead of time, and grilling them about their personal knowledge of what it might take to get a client to pay.

As he recalls it: "The whole system of collections was getting big enough that it could have been a separate company. It had its own computer program and filing system, as well as its own form letters and tickler files for phone calls; and it even generated its own personnel problems among my sales force. I was going nuts trying to run a collection company while running a surgical equipment and supply firm."

Finally, large overdue accounts with several clients merited hiring a collection agency and, later, a lawyer. "Now I had to keep track of not only the overdue collections, but also the professionals helping me attempt to get payment."

Harrison retained an attorney on a part-time basis to undertake all major collections work, while still sending the "polite reminders" out of his bookkeeper's office. "We've got a system and the right personnel to handle collections now; but we still collect far less than what is owed to us. The only reason we've been able to develop a stronger collection effort is because the firm has been wildly successful in its product line—way beyond original projections. Otherwise, we could never afford the time or money to collect on overdue accounts."

COLLECTION SOFTWARE

Many software programs are now available that are designed to facilitate your collection efforts. These programs are designed to give you instant debt reminder notices as soon as a bill passes the threshold period, which you predetermine. This helps to reduce the average age of your receivables.

Many programs offer several copies of collection or dunning letters that you can readily adapt and send. One program, called "Cash Collector," includes some 28 separate court documents you can use to speed up any legal claims you may wish to make. The documents and system are advertised as "legally sound," thus protecting you from harassment suits debtors may otherwise use in response to your collection efforts.

The program allows you to choose the order of the letters and documents that you want to send and then to preselect what days they will be sent on. It also enables you to add to your debtor's bill "a collection fee you're entitled to for the time and effort you spend in the collection process."

If you primarily bill for your time, *Timeslips* keeps track of different fee structures for different types of work and automatically prepares invoices. There are dozens of similar programs to help you keep tabs on your accounts receivable. Most collection support software programs also provide you with daily, weekly, monthly, or quarterly reports indicating who owes what, and since when. Consult any retail software vendor.

COST OF BENEFITS

Software support notwithstanding, some firms can afford to chase after collections; however, many cannot. Those with slim profit margins, which do not take these costs into account, are likely to suffer. Some issues to consider if you haven't firmly established your collection policies:

- How much capital will be tied up in receivables?
- Will I need to borrow against accounts receivable in order to remain in business or to expand?
- What will be the cost of this borrowing?
- Should I charge interest on past-due accounts? What will that do to customer good will?
- What will be the extent of our collections? Do I intend to "let go" when it means expenditures like attorneys and collection agencies?
- Who will handle collections? Are these people trained?
- How can I extend enough credit to attract customers without extending too much?
- Who will get credit? Who on the staff will review who gets how much credit?
- Will I do credit checks? How and with which staff?
- Do I want to offer discounts as early payment incentives?
- Can I get our own house in shape to process orders or give service more quickly, thus speeding up cash flow to its maximum possible amount?
- How will I limit problems that cause slow collections due to customer grievances with products or services?
- Should I offer lines of credit to good customers? Who will approve these?

The answers to most of these questions don't come easily. However, if they are not asked and answered, your firm risks some unfortunate developments.

Chapter 7: Hot Tips and Insights

✓ It's easy to get upset about the money others owe you, until you acknowledge that you have to train customers how and when to pay you. You either have a coordinated policy in place and make an effort to be paid promptly, or you've adopted a less-than-adequate approach to collecting what you've earned.

✓ The slower paying an account becomes, the more difficult it is to collect. A basic means of controlling bad debt is the credit application. Get the customer's home and business address, social security number, bank account numbers, and credit references—and keep the application current, updating it periodically for your old accounts.

✓ Managers who neither have to spend time tracking accounts receivable nor chase after late-paying or nonpaying customers are ahead of the game.

✓ To improve collections: Send out your invoices right away, reward prompt payers with an "early bird" discount, levy a surcharge on late payers, and encourage speedy payment by using the fax or electronic funds transfer.

✓ Include on your credit application a clause that spells out that in the event the account becomes past due, the customer will pay collection and court costs. To make this enforceable, include specific terms regarding late-payment fees on the application.

✓ A convenient method for verifying if a check is likely to clear is to call the bank on which the check funds will be drawn. While banks will not tell you specifically how much your customer has on account, they will tell whether or not the check will clear as of the present balance in the account at the time of call, less any amounts on hold.

✓ Investigate high-tech point-of-sale verification systems which verify checking-account and credit-card numbers.

✓ If a business account offers you a check, and days after you deposit it, it bounces, you have a number of built-in protections. Any check that you receive, whether cashable or not, is prima facie evidence of debt.

✓ If you receive a returned corporate check that does not identify the title of the signing party, you bring suit against that individual as well as the company. It's also useful to remind the bouncer that there are both civil and criminal penalties for passing bad checks.

✓ If you deal business-to-business, many collection difficulties can be avoided by paying the cost of obtaining current credit reports. For a fee, you can subscribe to commercial credit rating services that can supply you with detailed data about customers.

✓ With consumers you can obtain credit histories from consumer credit bureaus. This is the preferred way to give credit only to the most credit-worthy and demand cash from others.

✓ Ask directly for three or more credit references. This affords quick, verifiable information and can enhance other information you've gathered.

✓ Collecting breaks down into three stages: initial agreements, polite reminders, and aggressive strategies.

✓ The fax machine can be used in the collection process, if you keep the messages polite. If you know that the fax on the receiving end is in a "public" location, however, carefully consider whether using a fax reminder is appropriate for the situation, client, and sum in question.

✓ When accounts become overdue for long periods, say over 90 days, you may want to resort to aggressive collection strategies involving collection agencies and/or lawyers; however, they often mean losing customers or clients who feel you are being difficult and heavy-handed.

✓ Segment your collections based on how you feel about the customer or client, and approach them with either Kid Gloves, Shuttle Diplomacy, Boxing Gloves, or the Swat Team.

✓ Many software programs are now available that give you instant debt reminder notices. This helps to reduce the average age of your receivables.

CHECKBOOK TECHNIQUES AND TIPS

No man should accumulate money and not use it.

Robert Dollar

Check writing and check cashing are universally accepted business practices and an essential part of every business—this is certainly not news. What you may not know is that check use is increasing each year. Despite the long-standing predictions of a checkless society and the considerable effect that Automatic Teller Machines have had on check volumes, the use of checks has steadily increased.

In this chapter we'll offer ideas on checkbook management that you will want to implement, particularly if you run a small business, including:

- looking for a bank that pays the highest rate of interest while charging the lowest fees;
- keeping bank fees to a minimum by
  1. avoiding practices that add extra fees like writing uncovered checks,
  2. ordering checks from sources outside the bank, and
  3. using truncated checking;
- knowing what to do when faced with the problems of lost or stolen checks or forgeries;

- paying bills in advance of their due dates and keeping them with ready-to-mail envelopes in a file;
- paying more than the balance due on your accounts or paying early on occasion—practices that will benefit you in lean times;
- keeping a mini-cash-flow list in your checkbook and updating it for ready reference at all times;
- avoiding overdrafts and bounced checks by checking into the kinds of overdraft protection offered by your bank;
- following prescribed bank deposit procedures carefully for your own protection and always getting a receipt and checking it for errors;
- keeping careful detailed records in your checkbook and balancing your statement promptly every month; and
- using one of the personal software packages on the market for automated check writing and other accounting procedures.

Suggestions made in this chapter will apply to you or to whomever handles your checking account and generally apply to smaller businesses.

On the Rise.   Checks provide convenience and are inexpensive; they also provide the advantages of control and float (the time lag between the date the check is written and the time it is cashed by the payee). Check volume among businesses is growing across the United States at a rate of at least six to seven percent annually, totaling more than 60 billion. No decline is expected until the year 2000. Why are businesses using more checks today than ever before? For one reason, as a result of the AT&T divesture, most businesses now write *at least* two checks to pay the monthly telephone bill instead of a single check. Other reasons abound:

- More types of accounts are available (NOW accounts, Money Market accounts).
- More institutions are now offering checking accounts (thrifts, credit unions).

- More people are using traveler's checks and money orders.
- Although growth in the number and types of credit cards has replaced some check usage, multiple issues to individuals have created an additional source of written checks.
- Most consumers and businesses *prefer* checks.

CHOOSING A CHECKING ACCOUNT

The two basic types of checking accounts are interest-paying and non-interest-paying. It may seem obvious that an interest-paying account is the best deal, but before you "bank on" an account because it pays a high interest rate, there are several things to consider. The rate of interest you earn and the fees you pay on your account are dependent on your minimum balance.

The bank may charge you up to $10 each month the account balance drops below the required minimum. Your goal is to find the bank that *pays the highest rate of interest while charging the lowest fees*. Competition among banks is keen. If you've sleepily continued to use the same bank because it's inconvenient to change, it's time to wake up. Pay more attention to fees, since they can catch you unawares if you're not careful. Some banks may charge exorbitant fees in the one area where you are the weakest. Comparison shop by asking several conveniently located banks for their service-charge schedules. Look at what they offer at the minimum balance your business account can afford to maintain.

Curiously, and to your advantage, small banks usually charge lower fees than large ones.

If possible, use a bank with which you've dealt before. Perhaps you've built up a personal relationship of several years duration with a bank by having a personal checking account or a personal loan at that institution. If you find that fees are lower at a bank you haven't dealt with before, however, open your business account there and make an extra effort to become known by the bank's staff. It will pay off in the long run in the quality of service they provide you and your business.

Consider opening a checking account at a credit union, where interest rates are normally higher and fees are lower than at a commercial bank. Ordinarily, this is achieved by using the low-balance method to determine interest and fees.

CUTTING CHECKING ACCOUNT COSTS

Once you've chosen a suitable bank for your checking account, work to keep sufficient cash in it. A Consumers Union study showed that customers earned interest averaging $260 a year when writing 40 checks a month and keeping an average of $8,000 on deposit. On smaller accounts, fees exceeded interest paid.

If you run a one-person or very small business, put your business checking account *in your own name* rather than the business name. Banks charge more for business accounts than for personal ones. The disadvantage to this is that you must always remind your creditors to make checks payable to you.

Bank fees can take a bite out of your monthly cash balance. Here are some ways to lower fees:

- If you have several small accounts, consolidate them into a single, interest-paying checking account.
- Choose a minimum balance you can afford.
- Check with the bank on how soon you can write checks against deposits. Bounced checks can cost from $3 to $30 each.

Order checks from sources outside the bank. Many banks charge $15 or more for 200 blank checks, according to the American Bankers Association. Companies such as Current, Inc. in Colorado (1-800-426-0822) or Checks in the Mail in California (1-800-422-2439) charge much less for the first 200 checks and an attractive rate for reorders.

Ask your bank about truncated checking, wherein you will receive a statement each month listing the type of transaction, date, check number, and amount of every check that has cleared the account *instead* of the canceled checks themselves. Since this saves the bank check processing time and mailing costs, it will usually charge less for these accounts. Checks are micro-filmed and stored for a limited time at the institution. If you need a photocopy of a canceled check, the bank can provide it. In some cases, this service is free of charge.

Bulk filing of checks is another way banks can reduce bank labor costs and check processing. With this system, after checks are posted against customer accounts, they are stored in bundles rather than filed individually by account number. This also min-imizes risks of human error because employees handle fewer items and check signatures for checks only above a certain limit.

HANDLING SPECIAL SITUATIONS

Lost or stolen checks and forgeries are situations you'd rather avoid, but when they happen, you need to be armed with infor-mation on what to do. With lost checks, report the incident to the bank promptly. A warning will be placed on your account, and signatures on incoming checks will be carefully inspected to detect possible forgeries.

If you suspect that your checks have been stolen, first make a report to the police in the city or town where the theft took place. Then notify your bank, telling them the date, time, and place of the police report. A warning will be placed on your account. In some cases, you may be asked to close your account and open a new one with a new account number.

You are not normally held liable for losses due to forgery if missing or stolen checks have been reported to the proper au-thorities. The bank or merchant/vendor who accepted the forged check will be charged for the loss. In California, for example, you have 14 days from receipt of your bank statement to review canceled checks and report a forgery to your bank.

If you don't report within this time limit, you may be unable to recover losses from subsequent forgeries. When reporting a forgery to your bank, you may be required to furnish a notarized affidavit of forgery that would be used to bring criminal charges against the forger.

Stop Payments. If your check is lost in the mail or you fail to receive merchandise paid for by a check and you don't want the check paid, you can order a stop payment in two ways:

1. Go to your branch and fill out a stop-payment order, supplying information such as the date it was made payable, the exact amount of the check, to whom it was written, the check number, who signed the check, and the reason for the stop payment. The bank will verify that the check has not cleared before the stop payment is placed in effect.

2. Mail your bank branch a written request for stop payment. Your letter should contain all of the above information about the check and include your authorized signature. The stop payment will go into effect only when the bank receives your letter and verifies that the check has not yet cleared.

Should the check be submitted to the bank for payment while the stop payment is in effect, it will be returned unpaid to the person who submitted it. That person will be referred to you for the reason the stop payment was placed. Stop payment orders have certain limitations, and you should check with your bank for further information.

A service charge is levied for filing stop payments, and at most banks the stop payment order stays in effect for six months. One expert points out, however, that if you lose a check or even your entire checkbook, you don't necessarily have to stop payment on the checks, which can cost from $3 to $25 each, or more. You could instead, tell your bank immediately when checks have been lost. The bank has full responsibility for forgeries. Then maintain a keen watch for forgeries on checks as they clear.

Overdrafts and Bounced Checks. If you write a check for more money than is in the account, the bank will either create an overdraft or bounce the check. In the first case, the bank pays the check and deducts the amount from your account, leaving a negative balance. The bank will send you a notice of such checks, along with the amount of the bank's charge.

A deposit must be made to cover the overdraft and the charge. In the second case, the bank returns the check unpaid to the person or organization to whom you wrote it. It is then your responsibility to contact the person or organization immediately to say when you will make a deposit to cover the check for their resubmission.

Banks do charge for returned checks, as do many organizations. If the check bounces a second time, additional fees will be levied by the bank and possibly by the organization. Banks offer two types of overdraft protection to qualified customers.

1. One type involves automatic transfer from your savings account. By authorizing this service, funds will automatically be transferred from your savings account to your checking account to cover any overdrafts. Minimum transfer amounts and transfer charges vary among banks.

2. The other overdraft protection is backed by a credit card or loan account. When you write a check for more than is in your account, money is transferred into your checking account. That money is charged, up to your available credit limit, against a bank credit card or a loan account opened for this specific purpose.

Money transferred under the second plan may be subject to interest charges under the terms of your agreement. Some plans also charge a fee each time a transfer is made. Again, qualification requirements for this service vary among banks.

CHECK WRITING TIPS

You say you've been writing checks all your life. What tips could you learn that you don't already know? We're betting you'll find at least one new idea in the following suggestions:

1. Fill in *all* required information and blank spaces when you write a check. If a stamp is to be used for the name of the payee, have it affixed in your presence.

2. Fill in any blank space that is left over at the end of a line with a straight or wavy line. Failing to do this invites fraudulent tinkering on your check if it should get into the wrong hands.

3. For your own convenience, complete the memo portion at the bottom left of the check—it will serve as a ready reference later on.

Write out checks to pay bills in advance of their due dates. Then, keep an advance file with a folder for each day of the month. Place the check in a sealed, addressed, stamped envelope. Then put the envelope in the folder of the day it's to be mailed. This way the money is allocated in advance in your checkbook, and your bills are always paid on time. It also means that you don't lose interest by paying early.

Even if you have a cash-flow problem, this method of paying bills works to your advantage. You are reminded when writing the check that there is an overdraft in your account, and you know when you've got to put money in the account before you can mail the checks sitting in the advance files. This system alerts you to your current cash situation and what you have to do if there is a problem.

Once in a while, overpay the balance due on your accounts or pay early. This procedure will do two things:

1. give you a psychological boost when you see a credit on your next statement;

2. give you a good reputation with your creditors, which could come in handy in the future.

If cash is tight, you will feel freer to call up your creditor and say, "Things are a little tight this month. Would it be all right if I pay four days late?" If they see in your payment record that you sometimes pay early or pay more than required, they will likely be more amenable to extending your credit for a few days when you need it.

This is a good way to handle a short cash flow. Most people play the game of not paying *and* not calling. This is the worst kind of financial management. If you can't pay on time, call and explain the situation, giving your creditor a "by-when" date that you can pay.

Keep a stick-on note in your checkbook for an immediate reference listing what's coming in this month and what needs to go out. This provides you with a running mini-cash-flow list that you can refer to anytime. Update it every couple weeks, or days, if necessary. As payments come in or go out, cross them off the list and add new ones. This protects you from cash-flow surprises. Also, enter your IRS quarterly payment on your stick-on note a month ahead of when it is due. Then write out the check and put it in your advance file until it's time to mail.

Keep a petty-cash fund for small expenses. For small expenses like miscellaneous office supplies, parking, or incidentals, it doesn't make sense to write a check. You may want to set a minimum amount for paying by check, perhaps $5 or $10. For expenses under that amount, pay them from a petty-cash fund.

To set up a petty-cash fund, write a check for $50 or $100 payable to "Cash," and put the money in a box marked "Petty Cash." Always be sure to place a receipt in your petty-cash box to cover every amount you take out. When the cash gets low, add up your receipts and the remaining cash—it should total the original amount you put into the box. Then write a new check to replace the amount of the receipts.

CHECK CASHING TIPS

For your protection and convenience when cashing or depositing checks, there are some useful procedures.

As a safety measure, it's a good idea to write a restrictive endorsement, "For deposit only," followed by your account number and your signature, if you bank by mail or endorse the checks before you get to the bank. That way, no one can inadvertently direct your funds to the wrong account or use them wrongfully.

On the deposit slip, identify checks by dollar amount and the ABA number of each. The ABA number is a code developed by the American Bankers Association that indicates the bank on

---

Beating the Bill-Paying Blues

For one reason or another, most of us don't enjoy paying bills. Perhaps we don't enjoy the paperwork, or perhaps it has to do with the idea of giving up the money we worked so hard to earn. That can be doubly true if our cash flow happens to be a little short at bill-paying time. Here are some ideas which may help you develop a more positive mind-set about that dreaded time of the month.

Pay bills on time. It seems obvious, but bears repeating. Businesses who consistently pay bills late are not likely to stay in business very long.

Befriend your creditors. This may sound a little farfetched, but if you like your creditors, it is easier to pay them. When you pay your bills, don't think of your creditors as demanding or unreasonable people. They deserve to be paid for the products or services you asked for and they provided.

As you write checks, *visualize* your money traveling full circle and coming back to you in fuller measure than it is being paid out. Don't underestimate the power of the mind to manifest money in your life.

Write "thank you" on the bottom of your check. This is a way of letting your creditors know that you appreciate the goods or services they provided for you.

Figure 8.1.

which the check is drawn. It normally appears in the upper right section of the check.

Before leaving the teller's window, double-check all entries the teller has made in your bank deposit record to be sure they are legible and correct. If you are receiving cash back from the deposit, check to be sure it is the correct amount.

Of course, always get a receipt for each deposit. If you are depositing checks, the amount on the receipt is subject to verification by the bank. For example, if one of the checks in your deposit doesn't clear, or there's an error on your deposit slip, the amount actually credited to your account will differ from the amount shown on your receipt. Depending on your deposit, clearance and balance pattern, your bank may give you immediate funds availability which amounts to next day availability on funds. If you are depositing checks on a regular basis and have few, if any, bounces, and you would like immediate funds availability, talk to the branch manager or senior officer at your bank. This presents a good opportunity to making yourself and your business known to your banker.

CHECKING ACCOUNT "HOLDS"

While the banking industry did not originate the saying "no holds barred," it can apply to your checking account. So be forewarned and forearmed.

Banks sometimes place a "hold" for uncollected funds on the full amount of a check you deposit, or a portion of it. The bank does this because the check is: (1) for a sizable amount, (2) drawn on another bank or another branch of your bank, or (3) issued by a person or organization not known to the bank. A hold means you cannot use the funds until the check has cleared, that is, paid by the bank on which it is drawn.

The teller will inform you if a hold is placed on your account and the number of days it is to be in effect. If you make a deposit by mail or through the Automatic Teller Machine, you will be notified of the hold by mail. Too many entrepreneurs ignore this small detail and write checks against the newly deposited funds, only to have them bounce. Make a note of when the money will be available so you don't overdraw your account.

MANUAL RECORD KEEPING

Among the three most important words in check management are KEEP CAREFUL RECORDS. Recording all transactions immediately is even more important in business than for personal checking accounts. Writing uncovered checks in a personal account can result in a poor credit rating, but in business it is a lethal practice which can result in bankruptcy.

Good record keeping on a daily basis can go a long way toward making the monthly business of bookkeeping less painful. If you have ever sorted through a mangled set of checkbook records that received essentially no attention for several weeks, you know what we're talking about. Here are some helpful tips worth putting into practice in your business.

Balance your statement *promptly*—a cardinal rule in checkbook management. If there are errors that must be traced, discovering them early will save time. Report any irregularities between your records and the bank's records to the bank as soon as possible.

Balance your business books as soon as possible after receiving your bank statement. Because your checkbook record, the bank statement, and your accounting records are interdependent, it's important to keep up-to-date and make sure everything is balanced and in agreement. Don't be tempted to put off doing your books until next month or the end of the quarter. Errors are much easier to correct when they are discovered early.

Keep your checkbook record as detailed as possible. The more detail you include, the more time will be saved later. Always include the date of the check, the amount, the payee, and a brief but clear description of what the check covered. And be sure to enter this information when you write the check—don't trust your memory!

Remember to look at the face of each check to double check it for "alterations"—a $16 check can become a $116 check or a $66 check. This small but important task should be incorporated in your monthly reconciliation pattern and also adds a layer of security to your financial management. When it becomes a habit you will not only have a reassuring expenditure system, it will serve as a no cost insurance/audit policy. By making it known that you regularly double check each check you may discourage uncontrolled or unapproved spending, and it may also dissuade any internal parties from altering checks.

Highlight in yellow (or other color) checks that are tax deductible, such as charitable contributions. This enables you to find them quickly in your checkbook when doing your taxes. You may want to use several colors for different types of deductions.

Keep a separate running list of all deposits with a breakdown of the source of each check. If you have various income accounts for tax purposes or simply for accounting purposes, you will need this information. By keeping current on this each time you make a deposit, the information is readily accessible when you balance your books each month. Such information is especially useful if you offer several types of services in your company and you want to know how one source of income compares to another.

Keep a record of all draws made by principals in the business on a separate list for reference when you reconcile your checkbook each month. This is much quicker than searching through checkbook stubs to see who took his or her draw when. It also has the added advantage of providing you with an easy reference record of everyone's draws throughout the year—when they were made and how much—in case you need to refer back several months or even a year.

CHECK WRITING WITH PERSONAL FINANCE SOFTWARE

The variety of personal finance software products available today is the result of evolutionary advancements which have come of age. Although originally designed for home use, these packages are becoming popular as tools for small businesses. Software can provide nearly all the accounting help you need to run your small business. While it can't replace your accountant, it can make cash-flow management easier and less expensive.

In choosing a personal finance program, first identify the features you want or need. Aside from features, ease of use and cost are the two major factors to consider. Don't buy a package more sophisticated than you need; it will add to the cost and may be more difficult to use.

Under tax laws, the single-entry bookkeeping system offered by most software packages is all that's required for sole proprietorships and closely held partnerships. Double-entry accounting can be complex and costly for many small business entrepreneurs.

Two of the earlier popular software packages are Andrew Tobias's *Managing Your Money* and Sylvia Porter's *Personal Financial Planner*. Both offer financial advice and an outline for money management, and can be used satisfactorily for small businesses. A variety of newer, even simpler products, however, is now available that fulfills the needs of single-entry bookkeeping. These include *Quicken, Smart Checkbook,* and *Financial Navigator*. Others such as *Dollars and Sense* and *Dac-Easy Light* provide a double-entry system and are somewhat more complex to learn and use.

Most personal finance packages offer automated check writing. All checks are automatically entered in a register, and an automated bank statement reconciliation is provided. You may write checks manually if you prefer. Most packages also allow users to categorize transactions according to budget or tax categories. By providing reports to demonstrate how actual spending matches up with projections, they can help facilitate budgeting.

Users say that printing checks with such programs cuts down on human error and solves the problem of not being able to read someone's writing in the check register.

Statement reconciliation is an area where errors are often made, resulting in bounced checks, which becomes a way of life for some businesses. By making bank statement reconciliation easier, personal finance programs can keep account balances up-to-date and accurate, preventing overdraft headaches.

Though many small businesses turn to personal computers and personal finance software to help save time and effort, many personal finance packages are not necessarily timesavers. Intuit President Scott Cook says that their research indicates "most of these packages require 22 to 39 percent more time to perform financial management tasks than when the same tasks are done manually." For this reason, Intuit's goal in designing version three of *Quicken* was to provide a program that was not only functional, but a timesaver as well.

This was accomplished by a user interface that closely approximates the way things are done on paper. The check-writing option, for example, presents a screen that looks like a check, on which you must enter the date, payee, and dollar amount in the same places they would appear on a check.

Quicken 3 also makes it easy to complete checks that are sent

Personal Finance Software Packages at a Glance

Quicken 3 (Intuit)	Screens and procedures closely match what is usually done on paper. Handles accounts payable and receivable, payroll, and related taxes. Generates cash-flow and profit-and-loss statements. Doesn't process invoices. Single-entry. Easy-to-use, limited system that keeps it simple.
DacEasy Light (DacEasy)	Bare-bones double-entry system. Has chart of accounts, general ledger, accounts payable and receivable system. Does invoicing but not payroll or inventory. Screen prompts guide check writing and allocates to proper account. Precise but lacks examples. Good for sole proprietor.
Money Matters (Great American Software)	Double-entry. Replica check on screen. As you fill out check, prompts and menus help you assign expenses to proper accounts. Recurring bills can be paid each month automatically. Can schedule automatic bank deposits, print invoices, monitor inventory, payroll, balance sheets, and income statements. Primarily for small-business owner. Easy to use.
Dollars and Sense (Monogram Software)	Double-entry. Optional set of starting accounts for business use, but no accounts payable or receivable, invoicing, payroll, or inventory. Useful for monitoring finances, but not an accounting system.
Financial Navigator (Moneycare)	No invoicing, payroll, or inventory. Useful tool for investment counselors, but offers little to other small businesses. Expensive.
Managing Your Money (Meca Ventures)	Andrew Tobias's latest upgrade handles accounts payable and receivable, prints checks and invoices, and summaries transactions for 1040 Schedule C. Mini-database to keep track of customers and suppliers. Useful for some businesses.
The Smart Checkbook (Softquest, Inc.)	Automated check writing and bank statement reconciliation, as well as other functions. Somewhat complex.

Table 8.1.

out on a regular basis and will even remind you when checks should be mailed. Although it is somewhat limited, *Quicken 3* is a good choice for small businesses because its single-entry system is simple and easy to use. Other software producers, however, are quickly following suit.

Categorizing Expenses. Most small business users agree that categorizing expenses is a useful benefit of personal finance packages. This feature allows a company to quickly see how much is spent in each category and if it's spending too much. *Financial Navigator* divides categories by assets, liabilities, equity, income, and expenses. A single transaction can also be allocated to various categories. The result is that it's possible to see where expense money is going.

Some programs provide time-saving accrual accounting. When bills come in that aren't due until a later date, they can be entered as a transaction group, but no checks are printed until the due date. This makes cash available for use in other areas. Some packages also feature bridges or interfaces to other programs, allowing more detailed tax analysis and reporting capabilities. If you're considering personal finance software for check writing, choose a package that will grow with the business.

Following good checkbook management techniques in your business can save you time and many a headache.

Chapter 8: Hot Tips and Insights

- ✓ Check use is increasing each year. Despite the long-standing predictions of a checkless society and the considerable effect that Automatic Teller Machines have had on check volumes, the use of checks has steadily increased.

- ✓ When it comes to checking accounts, find the bank that pays the highest rate of interest while charging the lowest fees. Competition among banks is keen. Pay more attention to fees, since they can catch you unawares if you're not careful.

- ✓ Small banks usually charge lower fees than large ones.

✓ If possible, use a bank with which you've dealt before.

✓ Consider opening a checking account at a credit union, where interest rates are normally higher and fees are lower than at a commercial bank.

✓ To keep your bank fees low, if you have several small accounts, consolidate them into a single, interest-paying checking account; choose a minimum balance you can afford; check with the bank on how soon you can write checks; and order checks from sources outside the bank.

✓ Ask your bank about truncated checking, where you will receive a statement each month listing the type of transaction, date, check number, and amount of every check that has cleared the account instead of the canceled checks themselves.

✓ Ask about bulk filing of checks which is another way banks can reduce bank labor costs and check processing. After checks are posted against customer accounts, they are stored in bundles rather than filed individually by account number.

✓ Write out checks to pay bills in advance of their due dates. Then, keep an advance file with a folder for each day of the month. Place the check in a sealed, addressed, stamped envelope. Put the envelope in the folder of the day it's to be mailed. This way the money is allocated in advance in your checkbook, and your bills are always paid on time. It also means that you don't lose interest by paying early.

✓ Once in a while, overpay the balance due on your accounts or pay early to gain a psychological boost when you see a credit on your next statement, and to develop a good reputation with your creditors, which could come in handy in the future.

✓ Keep a stick-on note in your checkbook for an immediate reference of what's coming in and what needs to go out.

✓ Keep a petty cash fund for small expenses since it doesn't make sense to write checks for every item.

✓ Among the three most important words in check management are KEEP CAREFUL RECORDS.

✔   Today, software can provide nearly all the accounting help
you need to run a small business. First identify the features
you want or need. Don't buy a package more sophisticated
than you need; it will add to the cost and may be more
difficult to use.

9

CONTRACTOR CASH TRAPS

The winds are always on the side of the ablest navigator.

Edward Gibson

Let's face it, when you contract with another party to perform a service or deliver a good, unless you get some money up front, other types of assistance, or some form of assurance, you're at risk for your time and any out-of-pocket expenses. A growing number of managers recognize the necessity of not having jobs won turn into cash traps.

STANDARD TOOLS

You can seek many forms of accelerated payment, such as those that some suppliers may request of you. These include cash with order, cash in advance, and cash on delivery (see Chapter 3). You can ask for progress payments, based on the percentages of work done or at agreed-upon dates.

If you're working for a larger contractor, you can seek advances for itemized direct expenses. If your task requires hiring subcontractors, you could arrange to have the client pay the subs directly and bypass your having to serve as cash go-between.

When your accounts receivables are large and there is low risk of collection problems, you can approach your bank to get a loan on your receivables, or you can factor your receivables, whereby another party buys them at a discount and takes them over from you.

You can also work closely with the customer to ensure that you don't under- or over-stock your inventory in meeting their needs. You can save on overtime and equipment by coordinating order schedules with the customer. You can also work together to achieve cost-effective design changes, delivery, or distribution systems, and other opportunities to cut costs.

GETTING IN OVER YOUR HEAD

Cash traps among contractors frequently result from taking on bad business in the first place, or worse, not fully understanding the requirements of jobs they've bid on and won.

Requests for proposals, and invitations for bids issued by large corporations, the federal government, and other organizations and institutions require great attention to detail. In many cases, contract clauses are incorporated by reference only. The unseasoned, or overly eager contractor faces eight potential errors in bidding and providing contract services that will result in cash traps downline.

Failing to Closely Read All Parts of the Solicitation

A manufacturer in Fort Worth was awarded a $335,000 contract to supply parts for aircraft flight-recording instruments. After a significant portion of the work had commenced, and sample items were submitted to the contracting organization's representative, it was determined that a specified material had not been used in the manufacturing process, probably due to the entrepreneur's failure to read and follow the precise specifications.

Understandably, the entrepreneur was upset. He had already committed several tens of thousands of dollars to the project and was in mid-production when the error was first revealed. The entrepreneur sought to have this particular specification waived, which in some instances is a possibility. However, on this particular contract a waiver could not be granted because the material used by the entrepreneur did not provide the same level of long-term reliability.

In addition to losses in time and materials, as well as underused production capabilities, the entrepreneur also incurred legal expenses, added administrative expenses, and one long headache. Weeks became months before the matter was resolved.

A small manufacturer was the winning bidder on a contract to provide parts for shock absorbers, such as those used in automobiles. The contract called for several items that were outside the contractor's capability, but which he felt sure were of no consequence to efficient production of the end product. He had successfully produced a similar item a few months earlier and saw no problem in offering what was needed on a new contract, versus what was *actually* requested.

The first shipment was unconditionally rejected, resulting in the loss of several thousand dollars. Subsequent discussion between the entrepreneur and the contracting officer resulted in contract termination. Though the entrepreneur's cash losses were minor compared to the loss that would have occurred without early detection, the entrepreneur also disqualified his company from doing business with the contracting organization. Thus the incident resulted in a double loss.

New bidders must determine all that is expected before bidding and take into account the resources necessary for contract administration, handling extensive documentation, quality-control assurance, and reporting. A government agency's way of doing business, for example, varies widely from commercial practice. What looks like a cash cow might become a cash drain.

Unrealistic Optimism in Determining the Ability to Perform Tasks and Assume Risk

Those seeking a first major contract are prone to be optimistic in assessing their company's ability to meet the requirement and in assessing the possibility of things going wrong.

Sometimes, in an attempt to achieve a certain sales volume or profit level, entrepreneurs effectively blind themselves to the realities of handling new or large contracts. A Norfolk, VA contractor to the U.S. Navy was caught in a disastrous financial crunch when his suppliers failed to deliver on time and no backup suppliers had been identified.

Handling a large contract requires raw materials and increased labor expenditures. The inability to maintain a favorable working capital position has been the downfall of many businesses, just at that moment in which they were about "break into the big time" and execute on a number of unprecedented large contracts. The Small Business Administration offers the following questions to critically approach each solicitation:

- Is my staff competent to handle this job?
- If necessary, is additional labor readily available?
- Are my facilities adequate?
- Are my quality control standards and procedures in place and adequate?
- Can I meet all delivery schedules?
- Can I be budgeted tightly and stay on target?

Answering those questions honestly will help to reduce excessive zeal in taking on new contracts and the resulting cash drain that often follows. As standard procedure, it makes sense to develop a realistic approach in determining whether or not you have the overall capability, both technical and financial, to perform on selected projects. The expense items and trouble spots that you don't want to think about when preparing a bid are precisely those items that must be addressed to avoid cash traps on what otherwise are supposed to be profitable contracts.

Bidding on Unreliable Purchase Descriptions or Specs

You may be stepping on a land mine if the contracting organization is seeking a new product or service for which no previous contract awards have been made. You could be in a similar situation if contractors were used years ago, but the contracting organization has not sufficiently updated its specifications.

For example, you receive a request for a proposal that contains a drawing that is five years old. The last revision was two years ago. The odds are high that the required design involves many changes that are not depicted. Any contractor who doesn't question the contracting officer before preparing a bid is asking for trouble. If the drawing contains numerous footnotes and references, it is a good bet that there will be some peculiarities that should be discussed before a bid is ever made. Veteran contractors can often detect unreliable drawings. First-time entrepreneurs need to obtain as much advice and experienced input as possible before preparing a bid. Otherwise, you may be buying into someone else's blunder.

Similarly, purchase descriptions and specifications may contain ambiguous, confusing, or misleading information. Here is a particularly insidious vendor trap. A revision is made to a specification and the update is received but not placed in the file, not received in time to make the necessary changes and still meet the deadline, or received after a bid has been made. Most contracting organizations strive to avoid sending out late announcements, updates, or revisions. But it does happen, and you can't afford to suffer the consequences.

Another problem with specifications is the proliferation of different numbering systems. Associations, industries, the Department of Defense, the federal government, and state and local governments may all have different numbering systems for the same items.

What action can you take? Whenever needed or even presumed to be needed, immediately call for a clarification of unclear drawings, purchasing descriptions, or specifications. Also, be certain that any and all copies of dates of revisions to specifications are obtained and incorporated before submitting a bid.

Bidding on Estimations Instead of Actual Cost Data

The ABACO Company, headquartered outside of Atlanta, finds out the size of a federal contract award received by last year's winner. The president of the company mistakenly believes that by slightly underbidding last year's award price, his firm will be in the best position to win the contract this year.

To simply underbid last year's winning price is folly; your price may not recapture your costs plus a fair profit. Worse, it may not reflect the scope of effort required on this year's contract. Another frequent cash trap for contractors occurs when one produces a bid price using historical prices on comparable items rather than using updated market information on the current costs of the items, including materials and components.

Frequently, new or first-time entrepreneurs are so eager to get in on the ground floor with a particular organization that they bid low (to merely break even on the first job), hoping that this will lead to other jobs. This is a serious mistake, with cataclysmic results. The contract is won, but rather than break even, the business sustains a loss, and in some cases, a significant one. This, coupled with the inability to gain a quick, profitable follow-on contract, can leave you in a far worse cash position than you would be if you had not bid in the first place.

"But what about the experience gained in handling the contract, the relationships developed with the contracting organization, and the inside information gained while being close to the customer?"

These items are valuable, but not at the cost of losing money on contracts. The ability to effectively determine costs when preparing bids is one of the most important skills you can develop on the road to successful long-term contracting and the avoidance of disastrous cash traps. Price, quality, and service are what win contracts when competing with equally qualified firms. Key costs must be adequately forecasted when bidding, including

- overhead costs and trends;
- subcontractor and supplier costs;
- number of person hours, overtime, and the cost of temporary or part-time workers;
- learning curves for labor and salaried staff;
- material costs and associated trends; and profit or fee.

Always prepare cost estimates on a per-bid basis, never relying on previously prepared bids or assuming that standard cost estimates or ballpark figures will be sufficient. Never bid on a job for which you can not make a profit.

Bidding Under Time Pressure

We know of countless horror stories about firms that submitted bids without checking them thoroughly. One East Coast firm bid on a contract to make repairs to access ramps along the New Jersey turnpike. While submitting the bid on time, they did not allow enough time to carefully review all of the specifications, one of which required all welding be done by certified welders.

The firm was successful in winning the contract. In the weeks that followed, when reviewing this specification in detail, they realized their mistake. As structured, the firm was unable to meet the requirements of the contract without subcontracting all the required welding. The subcontract resulted in a whopping increase in costs of almost 20 percent. This resulted in a huge loss on this contract, *despite* efficient subcontractor performance.

A midwestern contractor in his second year had not taken the time to assemble cost-accounting records to accurately determine production costs. Confronted with a short lead time to respond to a solicitation, he decided to "go for it." The firm prepared a quick estimate based on educated guesses rather than actual data.

Subsequently, he won the award only to experience a large loss as the "educated guess" turned out not to be that well-educated. Honoring the contract severely strained the resources of the firm and threatened its long-term viability.

A relatively minor error in computation, when compounded throughout a bid and then multiplied by production quantities, can spell contractual doom. Often, under deadline, bidders either forego double-checking computations, hoping everything is correct, or erroneously believe that even if they did make an error someplace, it won't really hurt them.

A longer-term solution to the cash traps that may result because of bidding under too much time pressure is to maintain long-term monitoring and tracking of significant business opportunities. This sounds like a tall order, but the most successful firms do whatever is necessary to learn of lucrative contracts in advance.

To develop a tracking system, you'll have to foster key relationships with contracting officers, maintain appropriate industry connections, subscribe to key industry publications, keep an eye on the competition, and anticipate needs—a lot of work!

Accepting an Unrealistic Time Frame

Related to the trap above is the situation in which a bidder knows in advance that the time frame called for in the solicitation is unrealistic. Why would anyone bid to take on such hazardous work? One reason is the belief that "the deadlines aren't fixed."

Never accept impossible time-frame contracts to get a foot in the door. The problem with this strategy, in addition to problems discussed in number four above, is that many fixed-price supply contracts, whether with a corporation or the government, contain a default clause that enables the contracting organization to terminate all or part of the contract if the vendor

1. fails to make delivery of the supplies or performs the services by the date specified in the contract; or
2. fails to make progress so as to endanger performance of the contract.

When working with the federal government, for example, if you fail to deliver goods on schedule, the government may not only terminate the contract, but may also procure services from another contractor. Then you become liable for any excess costs that the government incurs when working with a second vendor.

The solution is obvious: If you can't deliver on time, don't bid. Yet, at this very moment, hundreds of business are submitting bids on contracts for which they will not be able to deliver and which will present them with a cash trap that will put them out of business.

"Beyond-the-State-of-the-Art" Contracting

Occasionally, corporations or government agencies seek creative and exploratory procurements that are negotiated with performance specifications. End products to such procurements may include prototypes, tests, and evaluation models.

In the case of a creative or exploratory procurement, you have to maintain close contact with the engineer or technical representative of the contracting organization to avoid misconceptions about desired results and "eating the project."

Open communication between the contractor and project engineer are essential particularly in the case when significant evaluation and testing is required over several months' time. Written monthly reports backed by telephone reports and on-site visits can help ensure that a "state-of-the-art" type of project does not meander into one that is *beyond* the state-of-the-art.

Firms eager to conduct creative and exploratory type projects recognize the need for highly capable, technically-oriented staffs who can carefully analyze solicitations to determine if projects are feasible.

Hesitancy to Take Remedial Action

A small EDP systems-installation and software specialist firm had just won a large contract with the state government to update and revamp the motor vehicle department's system for licenses and registration renewal.

Four months into the project, the contracting officer failed to supply information necessary to perform accurate system checks and, moreover, indicated that such information would not be forthcoming. Distraught, the firm's project manager was further told to proceed as scheduled, perform what tests he could, and "not to worry about it."

Not ever having had this sort of situation occur and not wishing to rock the boat, the company president made the decision to proceed. Months later, the firm incurred substantial losses because the system proved to be faulty. Had the missing information been supplied, as prescribed in the contract, there was little question that the system would have been up and running with no bugs. As such, the firm incurred substantial legal fees to prove it was not at fault.

Fortunately, many contracts contain provisions for resolving disputes. When dealing with the federal government, for example, a vendor may go to the administrative contracting officer for a ruling. If the vendor doesn't agree with the ruling of the administrative contracting officers, he or she could follow an appeals process.

With private corporations, frequently a contract will contain an arbitration clause that binds both parties to the ruling of the arbitrator. In any case, you need to have appropriate legal counsel available from the beginning. It is a cash outlay that will help head off much larger cash traps.

WHAT'S YOUR UNIT BREAK-EVEN POINT?

To estimate a fair and competitive price that will yield a profit if you do win, you'll want to perform a break-even analysis. The following will help you find your break-even price.

To determine the costs of production, first distinguish your fixed costs from variable costs. Fixed costs generally do not vary with changes in the number of units produced or sold. The cost of renting your premises, for example, does not change because your production doubles. Rent may increase over time, but not because of your producing more.

Total variable costs change directly with changes in the number of units you produce or sell. Variable costs per unit are constant; that is, twice as many workers and twice as much material produce twice the number of units of product X. Your total costs is the sum of all your fixed costs and your total variable costs.

Your total revenue figure is derived by multiplying price times quantity. If you sell 20,000 units of X at $20, the total revenue is $400,000. Profits are whatever is left of the $400,000 after all expenses are paid.

Figure 9.1 illustrates the relationship between costs, revenue,

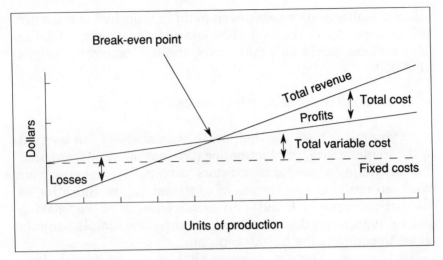

Figure 9.1.

profits, and losses in determining the break-even point. Knowing the number of units you need to sell to break even is important in setting the price. If you find that a product priced at $100 per unit has a variable cost of $60 per unit, then the contribution per unit to fixed costs is $40. With total fixed costs of $120,000, your break-even point in *units* is determined as follows:

$$\text{Break-even point} = \frac{\text{fixed costs}}{\text{per unit contribution to fixed costs}}$$

$$\text{Break-even point} = \frac{\$120,000}{\$40/\text{Unit}} = 3000 \text{ Units}$$

So, with a $40 per-unit contribution to fixed costs (hence a $40 gross-profit margin per unit), you must sell 3000 units to break even. Above the break-even point of 3000 units, in this example, the per-unit contribution to fixed costs goes to profits. For example, if you sell 3001 units, profit equals $40. Each additional unit that sells, above 3000 units, adds another $40 to your profits.

To calculate your break-even point in terms of dollar sales

volume, multiply your break-even point in units by the price per unit. In the example above, the break-even point in terms of dollar sales volume would be 3,000 (units) times $100, which equals $300,000.

$$3000 \text{ units} \times \$1000 \text{ Price/Unit} = \$300,000$$

As you might have guessed, break-even analysis can be used in the manufacture, production, or distribution of any product; it is not simply a tool for contractors. As long as you know your overhead costs, or the portion of overhead you're allocating to the particular product, and the variable cost per unit of making and selling the product, you can use the same simple formula above to compute the break-even point.

Hardware store owners, book publishers, automobile dealers, and a host of business executives routinely use break-even analysis as a measure of what volume of activity is required to remain profitable.

BAD BUSINESS

Beyond effective bidding and knowing your break-even point, there are other measures you can take to avoid the problems and resulting cash traps of taking on bad business. First, find other vendors or contractors who have done business with the clients or customers on whom you are calling to see what their experiences have been. It is not necessary to call upon direct competitors.

When in contact with a contracting officer, ask to see if the organization has a small-business representative, coordinator, or office set up particularly to handle the special needs of smaller firms. Also, review the organization's literature to see if they have a written or expressed philosophy regarding their relations with vendors. Better organizations often have well-developed policies that serve both them and their product and service suppliers.

A common pitfall is to continue to serve marginal clients or customers when it is clear that these accounts are more trouble than they are worth. Those who tolerate marginal accounts often say, "We can't drop them because we need the business." Yet today is the future that you were contemplating three years ago; if you don't take action now, three years from now you will still be accommodating problem clients and facing cash trap problems.

For every hour you have to work with marginal clients on marginal contracts, you gain three hours in satisfaction if you decide not to. More importantly, you create a clearing in which you can contract with better customers on better contracts. For survival, take on whatever keeps you afloat, but don't let stopgap measures become standard procedure. Cash traps aren't mandatory for contractors.

GOOD BUSINESS

Many large organizations who contract with smaller vendors are willing to take proactive steps to help the vendor avoid the cash traps inherent in handling large contracts. The Xerox Corporation has greatly reduced the number of firms in its supplier base while providing longer-term contracts that compel suppliers "to become business partners, and build confidence to the point where suppliers share what they have learned."

A survey of more than 1000 office-product buyers and their managers conducted by *Purchasing Magazine* reveals that at least 60 to 68 percent of respondents already had ongoing national accounts programs.

Many purchasing divisions are turning towards *national accounts* to take care of commodity goods, particularly in the area of office supplies, such as copiers, fax machines, typewriters, telecommunications equipment, desktop publishing equipment, image/graphic equipment, electronic data interchanges, systems furniture, forms management tools, and faster personnel computers.

Some corporate purchasing offices are turning towards blanket agreements with suppliers whereby one supplier has responsibility for all of a particular type of produce or good; systems contracting whereby a supplier supplies a complete system, including all interface or peripheral accessory parts; and stockless inventory, whereby suppliers provide quality control, warehousing, and just-in-time delivery services.

Life-of-the-Program Contracts.   Suppliers who prove themselves by contributing to value analysis, assuming responsibility for the quality-control function, or who indicate superior performance in terms of traditional measures such as price, quality, and delivery, are often invited to participate in life program contracts. A life-of-the-program contract essentially guarantees that a vendor will be called upon to supply a particular product or service for as long as the customer, generally a major corporation, has a prime contract.

For example, if an aerospace manufacturer wins a multiyear contract with the Department of Defense to design and produce an advanced air surveillance system, then a vendor supplying equipment in support of such a system would retain that status for the duration of the prime contractor's contract.

Suppliers who have successfully served in life-of-the-program contracts are also able to leverage such relationships within one corporation when seeking to obtain life-of-the-program contracts in other corporations. The obvious benefits to the supplier— larger, longer-term contracts with predictable cash flows and predictable revenues—enable the supplier to build a sound business by having fewer but more valuable contracts, and less concern about cash traps.

Chapter 9: Hot Tips and Insights

✔   When you contract with another party to perform a service or deliver a good, unless you get some money up front, other types of assistance, or some form of assurance, you're at risk for your time and any out-of-pocket expenses.

✔   You can seek many forms of accelerated payment, such as those that some suppliers may request of you, including, cash with order, cash in advance, and cash on delivery.

✓ Ask for progress payments, based on the percentages of work done or at agreed-upon dates. If you're working for a larger contractor, you can seek advances for itemized direct expenses. If your task requires hiring subcontractors, you could arrange to have the client pay the subs directly and bypass your having to serve as cash go-between.

✓ Cash traps among contractors frequently result from taking on bad business in the first place, or worse, not fully understanding the requirements of jobs they've bid on and won.

✓ The unseasoned, or overly eager contractor faces eight potential errors in bidding and providing contract services that will result in cash traps downline.

✓ To estimate a fair and competitive price that will yield a profit if you do win, you'll want to perform a break-even analysis.

✓ Other ways to protect yourself include finding other vendors or contractors who have done business with the clients or customers on whom you are calling to see what their experiences have been.

✓ When working with a large client, determine if the organization has a small-business representative, coordinator, or office set up particularly to handle the special needs of smaller firms.

✓ Review the organization's literature to see if they have a written philosophy regarding their relations with vendors.

✓ Stop serving marginal clients or customers who are more trouble than they are worth. For survival, take on whatever keeps you afloat, but don't let stopgap measures become standard procedure. Cash traps aren't mandatory for contractors.

✓ Seek large organizations who take proactive steps to help the vendor avoid the cash traps inherent in handling large contracts, through national accounts programs, blanket agreements with suppliers, systems contracting, and life-of-the-program contracts.

10

SELF-AUDITING
TECHNIQUES

To be rich is not the end, but only a change of
worries.

Epicurus

In this last chapter we will focus on auditing and self-auditing
techniques; that is, the variety of internal controls available for
handling your company's cash, checks, and other moneys.

Not many years ago a company measured its success by how
much of its product it was able to sell. Today success is heavily
influenced by the ability to keep costs under control and, of
course, to maintain a healthy cash flow. Volatile interest rates,
shrinking profit margins, and increasing operational costs are
causing many businesses to reassess and upgrade their internal
control procedures.

The need for internal control becomes painfully obvious when
you consider the alarming rate of employee theft among U.S.
businesses. Statistics reveal that 75 percent of all employees steal
at least once. More and more company executives are realizing
that prevention is the best line of defense. Micheal Aldrich, a
vice president and director of loss prevention in Pittsburgh, says
"In-house theft is everywhere, in any environment where a person is involved day to day with large amounts of cash or is
responsible for merchandise."

Embezzlement of cash, check altering and forging, and mis-representation are problems for all kinds of industries. For banks and financial institutions, the preparation of fictitious loans is a problem, as is churning securities for brokerage houses. And, of course, stolen inventory is a big problem for retailers, whole-salers, and manufacturers.

A few years ago, a survey was conducted to pinpoint the oc-curence of various types of employee fraud in different indus-tries. Since only banks are required to report employee fraud to authorities, data on employee fraud was derived from a detailed examination of fraud cases brought to federal or state courts. Seventy-five percent of the fraud cases identified involved the theft of cash, with a sizable fraction of those involving forged or altered checks. Fifteen percent of total cases involved stolen in-ventory, and approximately three percent involved the theft of property.

BILLIONS PILFERED ANNUALLY

In-house thieves are becoming more sophisticated than ever. With the speed and efficiency of computers, it's no wonder that high-tech fraud is the fastest growing sector of white-collar crime. By switching just a few inventory figures, computer thieves can steal thousands of dollars, without the risk of messy paper trails.

According to the latest findings by the U.S. Chamber of Com-merce, almost $40 billion is stolen every year by employees. In rough terms, spread across a workforce of 110,000,000 employ-ees, that's an average of $363 per employee. And, employee theft is escalating at about 15 percent annually.

As much as $200 billion worth of employee time is also stolen annually. No business welcomes this reality. To small business, employee theft can spell failure, and some researchers believe that nearly one-third of all small businesses fail now due to employee theft.

A Night and Day Activity. In 1989, a 12-year employee for an East Coast supermarket chain stole an estimated $250,000 worth

Figure 10.1.

of merchandise before he was finally caught in the act. According to the company's head of loss prevention, employee theft occurs frequently, sometimes several times in one month by the same employee. The size of the heists can range from hundreds to tens of thousands of dollars.

Retailers fear theft the most. Look around any department store and you'll spot two, maybe three, security agents. One may think they're hired to prevent shoplifters from walking away with merchandise. The truth is that these people are hired also to prevent the store's own employees from stealing merchandise. Security personnel themselves, however, sometimes represent yet another source of employee theft.

Retail employees, indeed, have many opportunities to steal. Some damage merchandise so they can buy it themselves for a discount. Others abuse discount privileges, maneuver getting paid for more hours than worked, or even steal from the cash register.

Whether you manage a retail store or believe that your employees are the type of individuals who might steal, you'll want to consider the variety of methods available to you to help minimize your pilferage and maximize your cash flow. By strengthening internal controls and developing fraud-defense systems, you'll reduce the threat of employee theft and go a long way toward improving the quality and efficiency of your company.

START WITH YOUR ENVIRONMENT

Before you do anything else, evaluate the quality of your business environment and the communication level within the company. Have you provided the best possible work setting given your company's resources? Do you encourage your employees to subscribe to the values of fairness, honesty, and integrity? Do they understand what constitutes theft within your company and the consequences for those who are caught? Have you published a code of ethics for your company and ensured its distribution to every employee?

By creating a principle-centered environment, you can make significant advances toward reducing your company's theft rate or the likelihood of its future occurrence. It seems simple enough, yet many companies never say word one to their employees about the importance of honesty and the severe penalties of dishonest behavior. Many experts agree that the quality of your relationships with your employees is an excellent indicator of your employee's theft level, as well as your company's overall productivity.

Not surprisingly, poor hiring practices are often a major reason for a company's high theft rate and subsequent failure. For best hiring results, don't hire someone in a hurry without thoroughly screening their references or having them complete a job application. As one loss prevention executive put it, you'll be "giving away the keys to the barn."

SPONSORING AN EXTERNAL AUDIT

You may want to sponsor an external audit particularly to confirm to creditors and outside investors that your company has adequately safeguarded their interests. Other reasons for having audits include to

- examine and verify accounting records and internal controls;
- provide a control instrument over record-keeping;
- study a financial condition over a given time period, i.e., through a review of balance sheets, operating statements, and statements of changes;
- better enable the acquisition of credit from banks and third-party investors; and
- pinpoint the need, if any, for financial guidance and consultation.

The basic responsibility of the auditor is to perform an audit to ascertain whether your financial statements were prepared in accordance with standard procedures. He would include a review of all internal control procedures, specific financial records, and legal documents. Normally, the audit will focus on cash and securities, accounts receivable, inventories, fixed assests, insurance records, contracts, liabilities, and equities, as well as sales, expenses, operating margins, and taxes.

The auditor will verify accounting procedures, evaluate check-writing authorization process, review inventory control and purchases of supplies, examine personnel record-keeping procedures, and analyze the method of safeguarding assets.

Following the audit, the auditor provides a standard audit report that includes two key paragraphs: one describing the nature of the work performed and the other offering an opinion based upon examination results. Opinions fall into one of four categories:

- Unqualified. This means that all criteria were used and no restrictions prevented the disclosure of any information.

This is, of course, the most favorable opinion that can be given by an auditor.

- Qualified. This opinion signifies that, during the audit, an auditor found a disparity in a certain account or transaction. The disparity, however, was not significant enough to qualify the entire financial statement as misrepresented.

- Adverse. This occurs when the auditor has not found the financial statements to be fairly presented.

- Disclaimer of Opinion. If sufficient information is not provided to the auditor, then he or she may find that the scope of the audit is too limited for an opinion. Obviously, this is not desirable practice on a company's behalf.

Because opinions on financial statements are rendered only with the support of related documents, auditors often do not give opinions becuase unaudited reports have been prepared by a company's internal accounting staff.

For unaudited statements, new guidelines allow auditors to provide either a "compilation" of financial statements or a "review of financial statements." With the former, an auditor compiles data provided by a company without actually doing an audit of the company's accounting records and hence can provide no assurance on the financial statements. The latter service involves some degree of investigation by the auditor so that he or she can make a statement of limited assurance as to the validity of the records. A compilation financial statement is less costly.

Since many small and medium-size U.S. firms can be defined as "non-public entities," they can also qualify for compilation and review services if desired by directors, management, and bankers to determine a company's current financial progress. You may want to investigate the possibility of these cost-efficient services for interim period evaluation, that is, monthly, quarterly, or semi-annually.

A Few Preliminaries. Before he or she begins, an auditor will want to meet with company management or a board of directors to become acquainted and to determine what is to be included in the audit. He or she will also need to determine the actual scope of the audit by becoming familiar with the company's accounting system and identifying any problem areas within that accounting system.

Audits begin with an engagement letter from the auditor that outlines the auditor's overview and nature of the work to be performed, as well as the fees involved for the work.

The audit process moves from a review of your accounting system and a discussion of who on your staff is responsible for daily accounting activities, to a review of several randomly selected transactions, perhaps using flow-chart techniques or internal control questionnaires. If any additional information is necessary, an auditor will usually request it at this point in the process. After several other measures, the auditor offers the opinion, a report, and a management letter.

In reviewing the final audit report, you may want to request an oral presentation from the auditor to complement his written statements. This meeting's agenda should include

- a discussion of overall audit results,
- a discussion of any accounting discrepancies,
- a discussion of record-keeping procedures,
- a review of possible improvements to existing internal accounting control methods,
- a discussion of management's ability to handle its financial affairs,
- a review of action to be taken by the company,
- a review of long-term accounting difficulties,
- a discussion of new accounting trends,
- a discussion of other services rendered, and
- a discussion of the overall performance and financial condition of the company.

Take this opportunity to immediately correct any discrepancies that may have legal implications and could, as a result, limit your company's ability to borrow capital. By all means, capitalize on the knowledge and resources of an auditor following his or her audit of your company.

Topics you may wish to discuss with the auditor or your company's own internal accounting staff, include

- the quality and level of accounts receivable,
- collection of receivables (i.e., is it fast enough?),
- physical condition of inventories,
- physical condition of fixed assets (i.e., age, quality, deterioration, maintenance, and replacement), and
- status of accounts payable.

SPONSORING AN INTERNAL AUDIT

As an alternative to the traditional audit, an internal audit may appeal to you. Some individuals within your company will feel that internal auditing is impractical and a waste of time. Because few, if any, accurate methods have been developed to quantify the benefits of an internal cost-control program, it is sometimes difficult for nonbelievers to justify the costs for implementing such a program.

An internal audit program can reduce the cost of the annual independent audit by reducing the scope of this yearly endeavor. It can also improve the level of communication between members of your company and any independent auditor. Often, even a less-than-complete internal audit program can be beneficial to your company's internal control system.

Put your audit objectives in writing. These should be reviewed by high-level members of your company, as well as members of your company's board of directors. You may want to install an internal auditor or audit coordinator who reports to an appointed audit committee. In this way, you can establish the independence of the internal auditor who will administer the program and delegate responsibilities to other employees, as well as provide an effective review process by an informed committee. It is the auditor's responsibility to highlight weaknesses and make recommendations for strengthening the internal control process.

COVER THE BASICS

It may seem apparent, but the most effective internal control procedures for you are those that take into account which employees are likely to steal and how they might do it. Careless implementation of controls can actually backfire and encourage would-be thieves by suggesting that you are not fully alert to the problem. Overly rigid controls can affect both productivity and creativity within your company.

As mentioned above, in most cases, employee fraud involves acts as basic as forging checks or stealing cash, inventory, and property. Some suggestions to help prevent these kinds of employee crime include:

- Provide equipment sign-ins. Over twenty percent of all office supplies go home with employees, according to the Office Supply Ordering System of Livingston, NJ. Monitoring the use of office equipment and supplies can help discourage employees from taking more than their share.
- Change locks. Limit accessibility to your offices by periodically changing locks on file cabinets and doors. Be sure to also change computer passwords from time to time.
- Protect assets. Obtain fidelity coverage or "dishonesty insurance" to ensure rapid recovery of stolen funds.
- Prosecute offenders. Overcome your hesitation to prosecute employees who have violated your company's rules on employee theft. Prosecution, insist loss-prevention experts, helps to further deter crime.

CASH CONTROLS

Reviewing your record-keeping system and related functions on a periodic, unscheduled basis goes a long way toward protecting your cash flow and minimizing employee fraud. As your company grows larger, don't allow this important element of the business to escape your own personal scrutiny.

In any record-keeping department, for instance, clerks can program computers to add small amounts of change to the price of an item and later deposit that sum into their own bank accounts. These same employees can also add fictitious names to your payroll to generate additional income for themselves or someone they know.

Cash controls can accomplish several small business objectives. These include

- Prevention of employee theft,
- Maintenance of positive cash flow without interruptions, and
- Elimination of costly mistakes.

Here are some control procedures to stem cash pilferage and diversion of funds:

Cash, Checks Handling

☐ Is a responsible official assigned to prepare a list of all receipts, both cash and checks, showing from whom re-.ceived and amount?

☐ Is this list made in duplicate on numbered forms, both copies signed by a responsible official and by the cashier?

☐ Are deposits made daily of each day's receipts intact?

☐ Are payments received electronically verified by someone other than the terminal operator?

☐ Are deposits verified with each day's receipts?

☐ Are all checks received stamped "for deposit only" and deposited within 24 hours after receipt?

☐ Is mail opened by a responsible official other than the bookkeeper or cashier?

☐ Are all employees who handle cash, merchandise, securities, and other valuables bonded?

☐ Are customer checks endorsed immediately?

☐ Are checks ever signed or cosigned in advance?

☐ Are supporting documents required for all signed checks?

☐ Are each day's receipted deposit slips checked against the day's list of checks and cash received?

☐ Are the duties of cashier or office assistant and bookkeeper divided between two people?

☐ Are definite instructions issued that the bookkeeper or cashier may not have access to each other's records?

Bank Statements

☐ Are bank statements reconciled by someone other than the person authorized to deposit or withdraw funds?

☐ Are bank statements received and reconciled by someone other than the person in charge of accounting?

☐ Are duplicate bank statements requested if errors, erasures, or alterations appear thereon?

Accounts-Payable Controls

Most managers devote sufficient attention to accounts receivable (cash inflows) but not enough attention to accounts payable (cash outflows). This is potentially a big mistake. By not controlling how payments are made to vendors, a company can stand to lose a lot of money. Here are some controls for tightening your accounts-payable procedures.

First segregate duties. Don't allow one person full responsibility over both accounts payable and accounts receivable. In other words, don't let the same person remove assets and account for their absence.

In one bank in which there was no segregation of duties, a customer service representative was allowed access to customer signature cards and held-over account statements and, as a result, had every opportunity in the world to steal, which she did.

Make sure the checks your company uses are used in numbered sequence so that each one can be accounted for easily. Tear off the signature corners of voided checks and write the word "voided" on each one. Also, save your voided checks so as to prevent misuse and to assist in financial auditing.

Don't pay an invoice without verifying it first! No business can afford to pay for merchandise it never received or insufficiently received. When checking invoices, make sure that: your entire order was received in good condition and/or the services were completely rendered, the sum on the invoice is correct, any extra charges are appropriate, and any available discounts are taken and calculated into the final sum. Also check to see that the sales tax is applicable and correctly figured into the total, and that the same invoice was not previously paid.

☐ Are employees handling credit memos and adjustments denied access to accounts-receivable records?

☐ Are ledger clerks in credit and collection departments required to switch positions at unannounced intervals?

☐ Are customers' unpaid balances verified at least once a year by the auditor or a responsible official?

☐ Are individual accounts-payable accounts balanced with ledger accounts?

☐ Are terms, prices, and quantities on invoices checked against purchase orders?

☐ Are undeliverable verifications investigated?

☐ Are bookkeepers instructed not to make arbitrary adjustments in customers' ledgers?

Accounts and Notes Receivable Under Control

☐ Are customer accounts regularly compared with receivables account in ledger?

☐ Are monthly statements sent to all customers?

☐ Are accounts reported as uncollectible investigated to determine whether the customer actually exists?

☐ Are past-due accounts periodically reviewed?

☐ Are notes receivable and renewals of notes authorized?

Avoiding Payroll Scams

☐ Are there time cards or other records to verify employee hours?

☐ Are time cards carefully checked at frequent intervals for erasures of dates?

☐ Are all employees paid by check?

☐ Is the preparation of payroll and actual payment to employees handled by different employees?

☐ Is the bank statement for the payroll account reconciled by a responsible official who does not supervise the actual preparation of the payroll?

☐ Is amount of pay and time worked reviewed independently at irregular intervals?

☐ Are all voided payroll checks retained for review and audit?

Controlling the Purchasing Function

☐ Are purchase invoices attached to checks for payment and the former initialed by check signers?

☐ Are purchasing and receiving functions separated in order to affix responsibility?

☐ Are purchases and sales invoices checked to prevent reuse or alterations?

☐ Are vendors' invoices stamped "Paid," and check numbers and dates of payment noted on invoices?

☐ Are all returned purchases properly supervised by a responsible employee?

☐ Are purchase prices verified to be in line with the market?

☐ Is additional approval necessary for excess purchase orders?

☐ Are receiving and delivery functions handled by different individuals?

☐ Are prenumbered vouchers used on merchandise transferred from stockrooms to sales departments?

☐ Are sales clerks required to initial the vouchers acknowledging receipt of the merchandise?

☐ Are prenumbered job requisitions used?

Inventory In Place

☐ Is a physical inventory taken on a periodic, regular basis?

☐ Are inventories in public warehouses checked periodically?

☐ Is the person in charge of the stockroom denied access to the inventory records?

☐ Is frequent physical inspection of merchandise made by a responsible employee not from the stock departments?

☐ Are requisitions required for all inventory withdrawals?

☐ Are inventory records reviewed with someone other than the one normally responsible?

☐ Are written instructions provided for counting inventory.

☐ Are summaries of year-end inventories double-checked?

☐ Are different employees assigned for purchasing inventory and receiving or disbursing?

☐ When a physical inventory is made, are employees outside of the department being inventoried used?

☐ Are the results of the physical inventory compared with the perpetual inventory by a responsible officer?

Ship-Shape Shipping

☐ Are prenumbered shipping tickets used on all deliveries?

☐ Are both the shipping clerk and the driver required to initial the accounting department's copy of the shipping ticket?

In General

☐ Are all employees required to take annual vacations?

☐ Are accounting methods and routines recorded in manuals?

☐   Are all important records physically safeguarded?

Don't wait for your company to fall victim to inside theft. Talk it over with your employees. Determine the best way for your company to install and maintain internal controls for the prevention of fraud. Otherwise, your company may suffer from what one loss-prevention executive termed "slow, seeping hemorrhage."

CASH TRAPS ARE EVERYWHERE

The battle to avoid cash traps never ends. Just when you've taken care of one cost area, another slips out of control. You have to be fierce in the allocation of every business dollar. You cannot afford to do less.

Chapter 10: Hot Tips and Insights

✔   Not many years ago a company measured its success by how much of its product it was able to sell. Today success is heavily influenced by the ability to keep costs under control and, of course, to maintain a healthy cash flow. Volatile interest rates, shrinking profit margins, and increasing operational costs are causing many businesses to reassess and upgrade their internal control procedures.

✔   An estimated 75 percent of all employees steal at least once. Prevention is the best line of defense.

✔   As much as $200 billion worth of employee time is also stolen annually.

✔   Evaluate the quality of your business environment and the communication level within the company. Have you provided the best possible work setting given your company's resources? Have you published a code of ethics for your company and ensured its distribution to every employee?

✔   By creating a principle-centered environment, you can

make significant advances toward reducing your company's theft rate or the likelihood of its future occurrence.

✓ Poor hiring practices are often a major reason for a company's high theft rate and subsequent failure. For best hiring results, don't hire someone in a hurry without thoroughly screening their references or having them complete a job application.

✓ Sponsor an external audit, particularly to confirm to creditors and outside investors that your company has adequately safeguarded their interests.

✓ As an alternative to the traditional audit, conduct an internal audit that can reduce the cost of the annual independent audit by reducing the scope of this yearly endeavor.

✓ Put your audit objectives in writing, to be reviewed by high-level members of your company, as well as members of your company's board of directors. Install an internal auditor or audit coordinator who reports to an appointed audit committee.

✓ The most effective internal control procedures for you are those that take into account which employees are likely to steal and how they might do it.

✓ Careless implementation of controls can actually backfire and encourage would-be thieves by suggesting that you are not fully alert to the problem.

✓ Reviewing your record-keeping system and related functions on a periodic, unscheduled basis goes a long way toward protecting your cash flow and minimizing employee fraud.

✓ By not controlling how payments are made to vendors, you can lose a lot of money. Don't allow one person full responsibility over both accounts payable and accounts receivable.

✓ Don't wait for your company to fall victim to inside theft. Talk it over with your employees. Determine the best way for your company to install and maintain internal controls for the prevention of fraud.

BIBLIOGRAPHY

Bennett, Stephen, "To Catch a Thief," *Progressive Grocer*, June, 1990.

Bryan, Marvin, "Twelve for the Money," *Personal Computing*, May 25, 1990.

Chelius, James, and Robert S. Smith, "Should Small Business Self-Insure Workers' Compensation?" *Small Business Reports*, November, 1988.

Dentzer, Susan, "Excessive Claims," *Business Month*, July, 1990.

Diamond, Sam, "You Can Run a Small Business With Personal Finance Software," *Personal Computing*, February, 1988.

Duis, Terry, "Internal Auditing: A Program for Everyone," *Healthcare Financial Management*, December, 1984.

Dunn, Don, "When a Bank Holds your Check Hostage," *Business Week*, August 8, 1988.

Edwards, Paul and Sarah, "Insurance Crisis," *Home Office Computing*, November, 1990.

Gilfillan, Ian, "Cutting Company Phone Bills," *Credit & Financial Manager*, December, 1983.

Gist, Donna M., "Management Reviews Options to Boost Check Processing Efficiency," *Savings Institutions*, January 1986.

Gordon, Marsha, "Employee Theft," *Independent Business*, July-August, 1990.

Hardy, Kenneth and Allan Magrath, "Buying Groups: Clout for Small Businesses," *Harvard Business Review*, Sept-Oct, 1987.

Jaffe, Charles, "Bad Debts are Worth Collecting," *Nation's Business*, May, 1989.

Lamaute, Denise, "Making the Most of Government Auctions," *Black Enterprise*, February, 1989.

Mandell, Mel, "Take Charge of Your Phones," *Nation's Business*, January, 1989.

McCoy, Adrian, "75% of all Employees Steal at Least Once, Experts Say," *Pittsburgh Press*, February 19, 1989.

McElhatton, Jerry, "Check Processing: The Challenge Grows," *Bank Administration*, June 1986.

Meier, Harvey, Ph.D., "A Discussion of Auditing and Small Business," *Journal of Small Business Management*, January, 1981.

Morcroft, Heather, "You Earned It—Collect It," *Charles Givens Financial Digest*, July, 1990.

Newman, Peter, C., "A New Way for People to Beat the Banks," *McLean's* (Canada), June 19, 1989.

Owens, Thomas, "Bum Checks," *Independent Business*, July-August, 1990.

Quinn, Jane Bryant, "Cut the Cost of Checking Accounts," *Woman's Day*, August 15, 1989.

Rapp, Jim, "Controlling the Cost of Medical Benefits," *Shop Talk*, December, 1990.

Silver, Pete, "Wring Your Phone for All it's Worth," *Home Office Computing*, April, 1990.

Snyder, Neil, Ph.D., et. al., "Using Internal Control to Reduce Employee Theft in Small Business," *Journal of Small Business Management*, July, 1989.

Stevens, Mark, "Self-Insurance Keeps Health Care Costs Down," *Small Business Reports*, July, 1990.

Wynn, Jack, "Quick Checks," *Nation's Business*, December 1989.

Further Reading

Alarid, William, *Money Sources for Small Business*. Santa Maria, CA: Puma Publishing, 1990.

Bangs, Jr., Donald H., and William R. Osgood, *Business Planning Guide: Creating A Plan For Success in Your Own Business*, rev. ed. Dover, NH: Upstart Publishing Co., 1988.

Berg, Adriane G., *How to Stop Fighting about Money and Making Some*. New York: Newmarket Press, 1988.

Berle, Gustav, *Raising Start-Up Capital for Your Company*. New York: Wiley, 1990.

Blum, Laurie, *Free Money for Small Businesses and Entrepreneurs*. New York: Wiley, 1989.

Brenner, Gary, M.B.A., J.D., Joel Ewen, M.B.A., and Henry Custer, Ph.D, C.P.A., *Complete Handbook for the Entrepreneur*. Englewood Cliffs, NJ: Prentice-Hall, 1990.

Brooks, Juliek, *How To Write A Successful Business Plan*. New York: American Management Association, 1987.

Cohen, William, Ph.D., *The Entrepreneur & Small Business Problem Solver*, 2nd ed. New York: Wiley, 1990.

Davidson, Jeffrey P., *Avoiding the Pitfalls of Starting Your Own Business*. New York: Shapolsky, 1991.

Davidson, Jeffrey P., *Marketing on a Shoestring*. New York: Wiley, 1988.

Forst, Brian, *Power in Numbers*. New York: Wiley, 1987.

Hodgetts, Richard M., and Donald F. Kuratko, *Effective Small Business Management*. San Diego, CA: Harcourt, 1989.

Luther, William M., *How To Develop A Business Plan in 15 Days*. New York: American Management Association, 1987.

McIntyre, William S., and Jack Gibson, *101 Ways to Cut Your Business Insurance Costs Without Sacrificing Protection*. New York: McGraw-Hill, 1988.

Mellan, Olivia, *Ten Days to Money Harmony*. Washington, DC: Olivia Mellan and Associates.

Philips, Michael, and Sally Rasberry, *The Seven Laws of Money*. New York: Random House, 1974.

Rich, Stanley R., and David E. Gumpert, *Business Plans That Win $$$*. New York: Harper & Row, 1985.

Seglin, Jeffrey L., *Financing Your Small Business*. New York: McGraw-Hill, 1990.

Simini, Joseph P., *Balance Sheet Basics for Nonfinancial Managers*. New York: Wiley, 1990

Special Reports

"A Guide to Checks and Checking," *The CIRcular*, Consumer Information Report 10. San Francisco: Bank of America, 1987.

"Risk Management: A Small Business Primer." Washington, DC: U.S. Chamber of Commerce, 1990.

"Small Business Risk Management Guide," Fort Worth, TX: U.S. Small Business Administration, Office of Business Development, MP-28, 1989.

INDEX